JAMES BALDWIN

JAMES BALDWIN
THE LAST INTERVIEW
and OTHER CONVERSATIONS

MELVILLE HOUSE
BROOKLYN · LONDON

CONTENTS

AN INTERVIEW WITH JAMES BALDWIN

INTERVIEW BY STUDS TERKEL
ALMANAC, WFMT, CHICAGO
DECEMBER 29, 1961

When it thunders and lightning and the wind begins to blow,
When it thunders and lightning and the wind begins to blow,
There's thousands of people
They ain't got no place to go.
My house fell down,
And I can't live there no more.

Bessie Smith, *Back Water Blues* (1927)

TERKEL: Sitting with me hearing Bessie Smith singing of disaster, a flood, is James Baldwin, the young American novelist. But perhaps a more specific description of Mr. Baldwin, since he is one of the rare men in the world who seems to know who he is today, would be: James Baldwin, brilliant young Negro American writer. As you listen to this record of Bessie Smith, Jim, what is your feeling?

BALDWIN: It is very hard to describe that feeling. The first time I heard this record was in Europe, and under very different circumstances than I had ever listened to Bessie in New York. What struck me was the fact that she was singing, as you say, about a disaster, which had almost killed her, and she accepted it and was going beyond it. The *fantastic* understatement in it. It is the way I want to write, you know. When she says, "My house fell down, and I can't live there no more"—it is a great ... a great sentence. A great achievement.

TERKEL: I'm looking at a passage in your new book, a remarkable one, *Nobody Knows My Name*, a series of essays,
articles, opinions. You say here that when you went to live
in the mountains of Switzerland you arrived armed with two
Bessie Smith records and a typewriter.

"I began to try to re-create the life I had first known as
a child and from which I had spent so many years in flight,"
you wrote. "It was Bessie Smith, through her tone and her
cadence, who helped me to dig back to the way I myself must
have spoken when I was a pickaninny, and to remember the
things I had heard and seen and felt. I had buried them very
deep." Now, here's the part, Jim: "I had never listened to Bessie Smith in America (in the same way that, for years, I never
touched watermelon), but in Europe she helped me to recon-
cile myself to being a 'nigger.' "

BALDWIN: Well, that winter in Switzerland, I was working on
my first novel—I thought I would never be able to finish it—
and I finally realized that one of the reasons that I couldn't
finish this novel was that I was ashamed of where I came
from and where I had been. I was ashamed of the life in the
Negro church, ashamed of my father, ashamed of the Blues,
ashamed of Jazz, and, of course, ashamed of watermelon: all
of these stereotypes that the country inflicts on Negroes, that
we all eat watermelon or we all do nothing but sing the Blues.
Well, I was afraid of all that; and I ran from it.

When I say I was trying to *dig back* to the way I myself
must have spoken when I was little, I realized that I had ac-
quired so many affectations, had told myself so many lies,
that I really had buried myself beneath a whole fantastic

image of myself which wasn't mine, but white people's image of me.

I realized that I had not always talked—obviously I hadn't always talked—the way I had forced myself to learn how to talk. I had to find out what I had been like in the beginning, in order, just technically as a writer, to re-create Negro speech. I realized it was a cadence; it was not a question of dropping *s*'s or *n*'s or *g*'s, but a question of the *beat*. Bessie had the beat. In that icy wilderness, as far removed from Harlem as anything you can imagine, with Bessie Smith and me . . . I began . . .

TERKEL: And white snow . . .

BALDWIN: And *white* snow, white mountains, and white faces. Those Swiss people really thought I had been sent by the devil; it was a very strange . . . They had never seen a Negro before. In this isolation I managed to finish the book. And I played Bessie every day. A lot of the book is in dialogue, you know, and I corrected things according to what I was able to hear when Bessie sang, and when James P. Johnson plays. It's that *tone*, that sound, which is in me.

TERKEL: This "tone" is in your forthcoming novel?

BALDWIN: Yes, yes, in a forthcoming novel.

TERKEL: Did you feel a sense of shame about a heritage that is really so *rich*, when you accepted the white man's stereotype of yourself?

BALDWIN: I'm afraid that is one of the great dilemmas, one of the *great* psychological hazards, of being an American Negro. In fact, much more than that. I've seen a great many people go under because of this dilemma. Every Negro in America is in one way or another menaced by it. One is born in a white country, a white Protestant Puritan country, where one was once a slave, where all standards and all the images . . . when you open your eyes on the world, everything you see: none of it applies to you.

You go to white movies and, like everybody else, you fall in love with Joan Crawford, and you root for the Good Guys who are killing off the Indians. It comes as a great psychological collision when you realize all of these things are really metaphors for your oppression, and will lead into a kind of psychological warfare in which you may perish. I was born in the church, for example, and my father was a very rigid, righteous man. But we were in Harlem—you lived, you know, in a terrible house. Downstairs from us there were what my father called "good-time" people: a prostitute and all of her paramours, and all that jazz. I remember I loved this woman; she was very nice to us; but we were not allowed to go to her house, and if we went there, we were beaten for it.

When I was older, that whole odor of home-made gin, pigs' feet, chitlin', and poverty, and the basement: all this got terribly mixed together in my mind with the Holy Roller, White God business. I really began to go a little out of my mind. Obviously I wasn't white—it wasn't so much a question of wanting to be white—but I didn't quite know anymore what being *black* meant. I couldn't accept what I had been told.

All you are ever told in this country about being black is that it is a terrible, terrible thing to be. Now, in order to survive this, you have to really dig down into yourself and re-create yourself, really, according to no image which yet exists in America. You have to impose, in fact—this may sound very strange—you have to *decide* who you are, and force the world to deal with you, not with its *idea* of you.

TERKEL: You have to decide who you are—whether you are black or white—who you are . . .

BALDWIN: Yes, who you are. Then the pressure of being black or white is robbed of its power. You can, of course, still be beaten up on the South Side by anybody; I mean, the social menace does not lessen. The world perhaps can destroy you physically. The danger of your destroying yourself does not vanish, but it is minimized.

TERKEL: The name of your book—this is directly connected— *Nobody Knows My Name.* For years you have been known as James but never as James Baldwin—"Home, James"; sometimes called George; in the old days, Sam; sometimes, Boy.

BALDWIN: Sometimes . . .

TERKEL: *Nobody Knows My Name.* Why did you choose that title?

BALDWIN: Well, at the risk of sounding pontifical—I suppose it is a fairly bitter title—it is meant as a kind of warning to my country. In the days when people . . . well, in the days when people called me Boy . . . Those days haven't passed except that I didn't answer then and I don't answer now. To be a Negro in this country is really—Ralph Ellison has said it very well—never to be *looked at*. What white people see when they look at you is not visible. What they *do* see when they *do* look at you is what they have invested you with. What they have invested you with is all the agony, and pain, and the danger, and the passion, and the torment—you know, sin, death, and hell—of which everyone in this country is terrified.

As a Negro, you represent a level of experience which Americans deny. This may sound mystical, but I think it is proven in great relief in the South. Consider the extraordinary price, the absolutely prohibitive price, the South has paid to keep the Negro in his place; and it has not succeeded in doing that, but has succeeded in having what is almost certainly the most bewildered, demoralized white population in the Western world.

On another level, you can see in the life of the country, not only in the South, what a terrible price the country has paid for this effort to keep a distance between themselves and black people. In the same way, for example, it is very difficult—it is hazardous, psychologically, personally hazardous—for a Negro in the country really to hate white people. He is too involved with them: not only socially but historically.

No matter who says what, in fact, Negroes and whites in this country are related to each other. Half of the black families in the South are related, you know, to the judges and the lawyers and the white families of the South. They are cousins, and kissing cousins at that—at least kissing cousins. Now, this is a terrible depth of involvement.

It is easy for an African to hate the invader and drive him out of Africa, but it is very difficult for an American Negro to do this. He obviously can't do this to white people; there's no place to drive them. This is a country that belongs equally to us both. One has got to live together here or else there won't be any country.

TERKEL: This matter of living together, this ambivalent attitude that the South has towards the Negro perhaps is most eloquently, perhaps tragically, expressed in the life, the sayings, of William Faulkner. His remarkable story "Dry September" seems to analyze the malaise, but, at the same time, he himself makes comments that are shocking. You have a chapter in your book dealing with Faulkner and desegregation. Is it this ambivalence, too?

BALDWIN: It's his Love-Hatred . . . Love-Hatred. I hate to think of what the spiritual state of the South would be if all the Negroes moved out of it. The white people there don't want them . . . they want them in their place. But they would be terrified if the Negroes left. I really think the bottom of their world would have fallen out.

Faulkner in "Dry September"—or *Light in August*, or even in *The Sound and the Fury*—can really get at (as you put it, "to the bone") the truth of what the black-white relationship is in the South, and how what a dark force it is in the Southern personality. At the same time, Faulkner, as a man, as a citizen of Mississippi, is committed to what in Mississippi seems to be their past. It is one thing for Faulkner to deal with the Negro in his imagination, where he can control him; and quite another thing to deal with him in life, where he can't control him. In life, obviously the Negro, the uncontrollable Negro, simply is determined to overthrow everything in which Faulkner imagines himself to believe. It is one thing to demand justice in literature, and another thing to face the price that one has got to pay for it in life.

No matter how Southerners, and whites in the rest of the nation, too, deny it, or what kind of rationalizations they cover it up with, they know the crimes they have committed against black people. And they are terrified that these crimes will be committed against them.

TERKEL: The amount of guilt here is a point you make very beautifully somewhere in *Nobody Knows My Name*. In the South, the white man is continuously bringing up the matter of the Negro; in the North, *never*. So obsessed in one case, so ignored in the other.

BALDWIN: It's very funny. It is very funny especially because the results have gotten to be, in the case of the Negro's lot in the world, so very much the same in both South and North. It must be absolute torment to be a Southerner, when you imagine that these people . . . even Faulkner himself was raised by a black woman (probably a model for Dilsey in *The Sound and the Fury*) . . . and one fine day, the child of three or four or five, who has been involved with black people on the most intense level, and at the most important time in anybody's life, suddenly it breaks on him like a thundercloud that it is all taboo.

And since we know that nobody ever recovers, really, from his earliest impressions, the torment that goes on in a

Southerner, who is absolutely forbidden, you know, to excavate his beginnings: it seems to me this is a key to those
terrifying mobs. It isn't hatred that drives those people in the
streets. It is pure terror.

TERKEL: And perhaps a bit of schizophrenia here, too?

BALDWIN: Yes, of course, schizophrenia. And not only in the
South. But the South is a very useful example, on a personal
and social level, of what is occurring really in the country.
And the sexual paranoia. It is very important to remember
what it means to be born in a Protestant Puritan country,
with all the taboos placed on the flesh, and have at the same
time in this country such a vivid example of a decent pagan
imagination and the sexual liberty with which white people
invest Negroes—and then penalize them for.

TERKEL: The very nature of the American heritage: the com-
bination of Puritanism and Paganism. The conflict.

BALDWIN: The terrible tension.

TERKEL: The terrible tension that comes as a result.

BALDWIN: It's a guilt about flesh. In this country the Negro
pays for that guilt which white people have about the flesh.

TERKEL: Since you bring up this point, I think, too, of the
position of Negro women and the Negro man. In the beautiful article you wrote for *Tone* magazine, you were saying

something about the white mistress of the house, who admires her maid very much, but speaks of the no-account husband. What does it mean to be a Negro male?

BALDWIN: The old, old phrase: "Negroes are the last to be hired and the first to be fired." This doesn't apply to the Negro maid particularly, though it can. It actually applies, without exception, and with great rigor, to Negro men. One has got to consider, especially when you talk about this whole tension between violence and nonviolence, the dilemma and the rage and the anguish of a Negro man who, in the first place, is forced to accept all kinds of humiliation in his working day, whose power in the world is so slight he cannot really protect his home, his wife, his children, when he finds himself out of work. And then he watches his children growing up, menaced in exactly the same way he has been menaced.

When a Negro child is fourteen, he knows the score already. There is nothing you can do. And all you can do about it is try ... is pray really that this will not destroy him. But the tension this creates within the best of the Negro men is absolutely unimaginable, and something this country refuses to imagine, and very, very dangerous.

It complicates the sexuality of the country, and of the Negro, in a hideous way, because all Negroes are raised in a kind of matriarchy, since, after all, the wife can go out and wash the white ladies' clothes and steal from the kitchen. And this is the way we have all grown up. This creates another social and psychological problem, in what we like to refer to as a subculture, which is part of a bill the country is going to have to pay. Bills always do come in.

TERKEL: A phrase Sandburg used: "Slums always seek their revenge."

BALDWIN: Yes, they do, indeed.

TERKEL: Thinking about the matriarchal set-up of the Negro family and Negro life—even back in slave days, the underground railway leaders were women, like Harriet Tubman.

BALDWIN: Yeah. It is a terrible thing: Negro women for generations have raised white children, who sometimes lynched *their* children, and they have tried to raise their own child, like a man; and yet in the full knowledge that if he really walks around like a man he is going to be cut down. A terrible kind of dilemma. A terrible price to ask anybody to pay. In this country, Negro women have been paying it for three hundred years; and for one hundred of those years when they were legally and technically free. When people talk about *time*, therefore, I can't help but be absolutely not only impatient but bewildered. *Why* should I wait any longer? In any case, even if I were willing to—which I am not—how?

TERKEL: You mean the point about "Go slow."

BALDWIN: "Go slow," yes.

TERKEL: The final sentences in your essay on Faulkner: "There is never time in the future in which we will work out our salvation. The challenge is in the moment, the time is always now."

BALDWIN: Now.

TERKEL: The world we are living in ... we have to make it over. We made the world we live in. You speak of now. It is always now.

BALDWIN: Time is always now. Everybody who has ever thought about his own life knows this. You don't make resolutions about something you are going to do next year. No! You decide to write a book: the book may be finished twenty years from now, but you've got to start it now.

TERKEL: I'm thinking of the subtitle of your book—and of the position of the Negro woman and Negro man—*More Notes of a Native Son*. Naturally, I immediately think of Richard Wright, who has meant so much to you as an artist and a man—

BALDWIN: Yes.

TERKEL: —his short story, which you refer to beautifully here in the chapter "Alas, Poor Richard," the story "Man of All Work," in which the husband, in order to get a job, dresses himself up in his wife's clothes and hires out as a cook.

BALDWIN: A beautiful, terrifying story. It really gets something which has been hidden for all these generations, which is the ways in which ... It really suggests, more forceably than anything I've ever read, the humiliation the Negro male endures. And it is this that our country doesn't want to know. And, therefore, when people talk about the Noble Savage, and the greater sexuality of Negroes, and that *jazz* . . . I could name six men with whom I grew up, who are on the needle just because there is really no . . . The demoralization is so complete. In order to make the act of love, there has got to be a certain confidence, a certain trust. Otherwise it degenerates into nothing but desperate and futureless brutality.

TERKEL: You've mentioned the needle; and we think of course of junkies and narcotics. For some, perhaps, it is the only means of escape from the brutal reality.

BALDWIN: Yes, that's right. I knew a boy very well once who told me, in almost just that many words, that he wasn't trying to get "high," he was just trying to hold himself together. He talked about himself walking through one of our cities one morning, and the way people looked at him, and he said to himself, he told me, "You ought to be able to bear me if I can bear you." What is most important about it is that all these things might not be so terrible if, when facing well-meaning white people, one didn't realize that they don't know anything about this at all. They don't want to know.

Somehow this is really the last drop in a very bitter cup. If they don't know and don't want to know, then, what hope is there? People talk to me about the strides that have been made—and all these dreary movies Hollywood keeps showing about "Be kind to Negroes today" and "Isn't this a good sign?" Well, of course, they've never seen these movies with a Negro audience watching them.

TERKEL: What is the reaction?

BALDWIN: Well, for example, in *The Defiant Ones*, a movie which I . . . I really cannot say.

TERKEL: That's okay. Go ahead. Please do.

BALDWIN: At the end of that movie, when Sidney [Poitier] . . . and he was very brilliant in that movie; he does his best with a rather dreary role; he does something with it which I wouldn't believe could have been done. Anyway, at the end of that movie when Sidney jumps off the train to rescue Tony Curtis . . . I saw it twice, deliberately, in New York. I saw it Downtown with a white liberal audience. There was a great sigh of relief and clapping: they felt that this was a very noble gesture on the part of a very noble black man. And I suppose, in a way, it was.

Then I saw it Uptown. When Sidney jumped off the train, there was a tremendous roar of *fury* from the audience, with which, I must say, I agreed. They told Sidney, "Get back on the train, you fool." In any case, why in the world should he go back to the chain gang, when they were obviously going to be separated again: it's still a Jim Crow chain gang.

What's the movie supposed to prove? What the movie is designed to prove, really, to white people, is that Negroes are going to forgive them for their crimes, and that somehow they are going to escape scot-free. Now, I am not being vengeful at all when I say this . . . because I'd hate to see the nightmare begin all over again, with shoes on the other foot. But I'm talking about a human fact. The human fact is this: that

one cannot escape anything one has done. One has got to pay
for it. You either pay for it willingly or pay for it unwillingly.

TERKEL: That Negro audience shouting, "Get back on the
train, you fool" . . . we think of two movements happening
simultaneously with the Negro in America today: the Black
Muslim movement and Martin Luther King. Isn't there a direct connection here, Jim?

BALDWIN: Yes, yes, precisely. And I must admit that there is
a great ambivalence in myself. For example, I'm devoted to
King and I worked with CORE and tried to raise money for
the Freedom Riders. I adore those children. I have a tremendous respect for them. Yet, at the same time, in talking to very
different people, somewhat older, and also talking to ex-sit-in
students who said, "No, I simply can't take it anymore . . .": I
don't know.

 Let me put it in another way: King's influence in the
South is tremendous, but his influence in the North is slight,
and the North doesn't talk about the South. Chicagoans talk
about Mississippi as though they had no South Side. White
people in New York talk about Alabama as though they had
no Harlem. To ignore what is happening in their own back-
yard is a great device on the part of the white people. Whether
I were for or against violence is absolutely irrelevant. The question that really obsesses me today is not whether or not I like
violence, or whether or not you like it—unless the situation
is ameliorated, and very, very quickly, there *will* be violence.
There will be violence (and of this I am as convinced as I am
that I am sitting in this chair) one day in Birmingham. And

it won't be the fault of the Negroes in Birmingham. It is the fault of the administration of Birmingham, and the apathy of Washington. An intolerable situation. It has been intolerable for one hundred years.

I can't . . . I really cannot tell my nephew or my brother— my nephew is fourteen, my brother is a grown man—I can't tell my nephew that if someone hits him he shouldn't hit back. I really cannot tell him that. And I can still less tell my brother that, if someone comes to his house with a gun, he should let him in, and allow him to do what he wants with his children and his wife. But the point is: even if I were able to tell my brother he should, there is absolutely no guarantee that my brother will, and I can't blame him.

It is too easy, in another way, for the country to sit in admiration before the sit-in students, because it doesn't cost them anything. They have no idea what it costs those kids to go through that picketed building, for example, where people upstairs are spitting down on your head or trying to vomit down on you. This is a tremendous amount to demand of people who are technically free, in a free country, which is supposed to be the leader of the West.

It seems to me a great cowardice on the part of the public to expect that it is going to be saved by a handful of children, for whom they refuse to be responsible.

TERKEL: It's so much more easy, say, for a Black Muslim speaker to win followers than a Martin Luther King . . .

BALDWIN: It is always much easier, obviously, to—how can I put this?—to . . . Well, in Harlem, those Black Muslim meetings every Saturday night, and people there listening to those speeches, and all kinds of other speeches, because they *are* in despair. They don't believe—and this is the most dangerous thing that has happened—they don't believe . . . They've been betrayed so often and by so many people, not all of them white, that they don't believe the country really means what it says, and there is nothing in the record to indicate that the country means what it says.

Now, when they are told that they are better than white people, it is a perfectly inevitable development. Through all of these hundreds of years, white people going around saying they are better than anybody else, sooner or later they were bound to create a counterweight (especially with Africa on the stage of the world now): which is simply to take the whole legend of Western history—and its entire theology, changing one or two pronouns, and transferring it from Jerusalem to Islam, just this small change—and turn it all against the white world. The white world can't do anything about this, can't call down the Muslim leaders, or anybody else on this, until they are willing to face their own history.

TERKEL: How does all this, then, connect with being a Negro artist? Coming back to a man who meant so much to you, Richard Wright: he escaped. He spoke of Paris as a refuge. You looked upon it as a sort of way-station.

BALDWIN: In the beginning, I must admit, I looked on Paris as a refuge, too. I never intended to come back to this country. I lived there so long, I got to know a great deal about Paris.

Several things happened to me: one of them was watching

American Negroes there, who, so to speak, dragged Mississippi across the ocean with them and were operating now in
a vacuum. I myself carried all my social habits to Paris with
me, where they were not needed. It took me a long time to
learn how to do without them. And this complex frightened
me very much.

But more important than that, perhaps, was the relationship between American Negroes and Africans and Alge-
rians in Paris, who belonged to France. It didn't demand any
spectacular degree of perception to realize that I was treated,
insofar as I was noticed at all, differently from them because I
had an American passport. I may not have liked this fact: but
it was a fact. And I could see very well that if I were an Alge-
rian, I would not have been living in the same city in which I
imagined myself to be living as Jimmy Baldwin; or if I were an
African, it would have been a very different city to me.

And also I began to see that the West—the entire West—
is changing, is breaking up; and that its power over *me*, and
over Africans, was gone. And would never come again. So
then it seemed that exile was another way of being in Limbo.

I suppose finally the most important thing was that I
am a writer. That sounds grandiloquent, but the truth is that
I don't think that, seriously speaking, anybody in his right
mind would want to be a writer. But you do discover that
you are a writer and then you haven't got any choice. You
live that life or you won't live any. And I am an American
writer. This country is my subject. And in working out my
forthcoming novel, I began to realize that the New York I
was trying to describe was the New York which, by this time,
was nearly twenty years old. I had to come back to check

my impressions, and, as it turned out, to be stung again, to look at it again, bear it again, and to be reconciled to it again.

Now, I imagine, I will have to spend the rest of my life as a kind of transatlantic commuter. At some point when I'm in this country, I always get to the place where I realize that I don't see it very clearly, because it is very exhausting—after all, you do spend twenty-four hours a day resisting and resenting it, trying to keep a kind of equilibrium in it—so that I suppose I'll keep going away and coming back.

TERKEL: You feel your years in Europe afforded you more of a perspective?

BALDWIN: I began to see this country for the first time. If I hadn't gone away, I would never have been able to see it; and if I was unable to see it, I would never have been able to forgive it.

I'm not mad at this country anymore: I am very worried about it. I'm not worried about the Negroes in the country even, so much as I am about the country. The country doesn't know what it has done to Negroes. And the country has no notion whatever—and this is disastrous—of what it has done to itself. North and South have yet to assess the price they pay for keeping the Negro in his place; and, to my point of view, it shows in every single level of our lives, from the most public to the most private.

TERKEL: Can we expand a bit on this, Jim—what the country has done to itself?

BALDWIN: One of the reasons, for example, I think that our youth is so badly educated—and it is inconceivably badly educated—is because education demands a certain daring, a certain independence of mind. You have to teach some people to think; and in order to teach some people to think, you have to teach them to think about everything. There mustn't be something they cannot think about. If there is one thing they cannot think about, very shortly they can't think about anything.

Now, there is always something in this country, of course, one cannot think about—the Negro. This may seem like a very subtle argument, but I don't think so. Time will prove the connection between the level of the lives we lead and the extraordinary endeavor to avoid black men. It shows in our public life.

When I was living in Europe, it occurred to me that what Americans in Europe did not know about Europeans is precisely what they did not know about me; and what Americans today don't know about the rest of the world, like Cuba or Africa, is what they don't know about me. The incoherent, totally incoherent, foreign policy of this country is a reflection of the incoherence of the private lives here.

TERKEL: So we don't even know our own names?

BALDWIN: No, we don't. This is the whole point. And I suggest this: that in order to learn your name, you are going to have to learn mine. In a way, the American Negro is *the* key figure in this country; and if you don't face him, you will never face anything.

TERKEL: If I don't know your name, I, a white man, will never know mine. I'm thinking of Africa, and of how you have come home again by returning to your work here. Even though I have said that *Nobody Knows My Name* is a collection of essays, it isn't that; it is a novel; it is an autobiography, in a way. In it you wrote a journalistic report, very accurate and astute, "Princes and Powers." You were covering a meeting of Negro writers of the world. African writers, too, were speaking . . .

BALDWIN: It was really an African conference. Predominantly African. The Negroes were there as Africans, or, well, as the black people of the world, let's put it that way.

TERKEL: What of the African writer? Isn't there a problem here: the uncovering of this rich heritage, so long buried by kidnappers and colonial people, while at the same time technological advances are taking place, slums are being cleared.

BALDWIN: The twentieth century, in fact.

TERKEL: Yes. Isn't there loss as well as gain here? It is a question of things happening at the same time.

BALDWIN: It is a very great question. It is almost impossible to assess what was lost, which makes it impossible to assess what is gained. How can I put this? In a way, I almost envy African writers because there is so much to excavate, and because their relationship to the world—at least from my vantage point, I may be wrong—seems much more *direct* than mine can ever be. But, God knows, the colonial experience destroyed so much, blasted so much, and, of course, changed forever the African personality. One doesn't know what there really was on the other side of the Flood. It will take generations before that past can be reestablished and, in fact, used.

At the same time, of course, all of the African nations are under the obligation, the necessity, of moving into the twentieth century, and really, sometimes, at a fantastic rate of speed. This is the only way they can survive. And, of course, all Africans, whether they know it or not, have endured the European experience, and have been stained and changed by the European standards; and in a curious way the unification of Africans, as far as it can be said to exist, is a white invention.

The only thing that really unites all black men everywhere is, as far as I can tell, the fact that white men are on their necks. What I'm curious about is what will happen when this is no longer true. For the first time in the memory of anybody living, black men have their destinies in their own hands. What will come out then, what the problems and tensions and terrors will be then, is a very great, a very loaded question.

I think that if we were more honest here, we could do a great deal to aid in this transition, because we have an advantage, which we seem to consider to be a disadvantage, over all the other Western nations. We have created—no other nation has—a black man who belongs, who is a part of the West. In distinction to Belgium or any other European power, we had our slaves on the mainland. No matter how we deny it, we couldn't avoid a human involvement with them, which we have almost perished in denying, but which is nevertheless there.

Now, if we could turn about and face this, we would have a tremendous advantage in the world today. As long as we don't, there isn't much hope for the West. How can I put this? If one could accept the fact that it is no longer important to be white, it would begin to cease to be important to be black. If we could accept the fact that no nation with twenty million black people in it for so long and with such a depth of involvement, that no nation under these circumstances can be called a white nation, this would be a great achievement, and it would change a great many things.

TERKEL: Assuming that sanity ... assuming that humanity itself, the humanity in all of us, will triumph, there will be, as you say, no white nation and no black nation but nations of people. Now we come to the question of this long-buried Negro heritage. At the beginning of this interview, a Bessie Smith record was played. Once upon a time, you were ashamed of it. Now you realize that there is a great pride here—and artistry. Thinking now of the young African: if a certain identity, imposed from the outside, is lost, will he reject that which was uniquely his in the beginning for a grayness, even though it be more materially advanced?

BALDWIN: I have a tendency to doubt it; but, of course, there is no way of knowing. Judging only from my very limited experience in Paris with a few Africans, my tendency is to doubt it. I think the real impulse is to excavate that heritage at no matter what cost, and bring it into the present. This is a very sound idea. It is needed. In all the things that were destroyed by Europe, which will never really be put in place again, still, in that rubble, there is something of very, very great value, not only for Africans, but for all of us.

We are living at a moment like that moment when Constantine became a Christian. All of the standards for which the Western world has lived so long are in the process of breakdown and revision; and a kind of passion, and beauty, and joy, which was in the world before and has been buried so long, has got to come back.

TERKEL: Now we come to the matter of dehumanization, don't we: the impersonality of our time?

BALDWIN: Yes, yes. Obviously this cannot—I would hate to see it—continue. I don't ever intend to make my peace with such a world; there is so much that's more important than Cadillacs, Frigidaires, and IBM machines. No. And precisely one of the things wrong with this country is this notion that IBM machines and Cadillacs *prove* something.

People always tell me how many Negroes bought Cadillacs last year. This *terrifies* me. I always wonder: Do you think this is what the country is for? Do you really think this is why I came here, this is why I suffered, this is what I would die for? A lousy Cadillac?

TERKEL: That holds for white or black, doesn't it?

BALDWIN: For white or black, yes, exactly. I think the country has to find out what it means by freedom. Freedom is a very dangerous thing. Anything else is disastrous. But freedom is dangerous. You've got to make choices. You've got to make very dangerous choices. You've got to be taught that your life is in your hands.

TERKEL: The matter of freedom leads to another chapter in your book, in which you discuss a meeting with Ingmar Bergman, whom you described as a free, a relatively free, artist. Would you mind telling us about that?

BALDWIN: Well, part of Bergman's freedom, of course, is purely economical. It is based on the social and economic structure of Sweden. He hasn't got to worry about money for his films, which is a very healthy thing for him. But on another level, he impressed me as being free because—and this is a great paradox about freedom—he'd accepted his limitations: limitations within himself, limitations within his society. I don't mean that he necessarily accepted *all* these limitations, or that he was passive in the face of them. But he recognized that he was Ingmar Bergman, could do some things and could not do some others, and was not going to live forever; he recognized something that people in this country have a great deal of trouble recognizing: that life is very difficult, very difficult for anybody, anybody born.

People cannot be free until they recognize this. Bessie Smith was much freer—onerous and terrible as this may sound—much freer than the people who murdered her or let her die. Big Bill Broonzy, too—a much freer man than the success-ridden people running around on Madison Avenue today. If you can accept the worst, as someone once said to me, then you can see the best; but if you think life is a great, big, glorious plum pudding, you know, you'll end up in the madhouse.

TERKEL: To perhaps even extend the example you just offered: the little girl who walked into the Little Rock School House and was spat on was much freer than the white child who sat there with a misconceived notion.

BALDWIN: Well, I think the proof that Negroes are much stronger in the South today is simply . . . you know . . .

TERKEL: She knew who she was . . .

BALDWIN: She knew who she was. She *knew* who she was. After all, that child has been coming for a very long time. She didn't come out of nothing. Negro families are able to produce such children; whereas the fact that the good white people of the South have yet to make an appearance proves something awful about the moral state of the South. Those people in Tallahassee who are never in the streets when the mobs are there—why aren't they? It's their town, too!

TERKEL: What about someone like Lillian Smith [writer, magazine editor, and social critic]?

BALDWIN: Lillian Smith is a very great, and heroic, and very lonely figure. Obviously. She has very few friends in that little hamlet in Georgia where she carries on so gallantly. She has paid a tremendous price for trying to do what she thinks is right. And the price is terribly, terribly high. The only way the price can become a little bit less is for more people to do it.

TERKEL: This leads to what you wrote in your chapter, "In Search of a Majority," about the question of majority and minority.

BALDWIN: The majority is usually—I hate to say this—wrong. There is a great confusion in this country about that.

TERKEL: Ibsen's *An Enemy of the People* . . . ?

BALDWIN: Yes. I really think, seriously, that there is a division of labor in the world. Let me put it this way: there are so many things I am not good at—I can't drive a truck; I can't run a bank. Well, all right—other people have to do that. In a way, they are responsible for me; and I am responsible to them.

My responsibility to them is to try to tell the truth as I see it—not so much about my private life, as about *their* private lives. So that there is in the world a standard, you know, for *all* of us, which will get you through your troubles. Your troubles are always coming. And Cadillacs don't get you through. And neither do psychiatrists, incidentally. All that gets you through it, really, is some faith in life, which is not so easy to achieve.

Now, when we talk about majorities and minorities, I always have the feeling that this country is talking about a popularity contest in which everybody works together, you know, towards some absolutely hideously material end. But in truth, I think that all the Southern politicians have failed their responsibility to the white people of the South. *Somebody* in the South must know that obviously the status quo cannot exist another hundred years. The politicians' real responsibility is to prepare the people who are now forming those mobs, prepare those people for their day: to minimize the damage to *them*.

The majority rule in the South is not a majority rule at all. It's a mob rule. And what these mobs fill is a moral vacuum, which is created by the lack of a leader. This is the way the world is, and I am not talking about dictatorships.

TERKEL: Statesmen?

BALDWIN: Statesmen, exactly. People who are sitting in government are supposed to know more about government than people who are driving trucks, and digging potatoes, and trying to raise their children. That's what you are in office for.

TERKEL: Someone, then, with a sense of history?

BALDWIN: That is precisely what we don't have here. If you don't know what happened behind you, you've no idea of what is happening around you.

TERKEL: Earlier, Jim, you mentioned that for a national policy to be straightened out, the private policies, these private, individual lives must be, too. You spoke of your job as a writer, and of how you've got to write. In that chapter on Bergman, "The Northern Protestant," is a beautiful comment:

"All art is a kind of confession, more or less oblique. All artists, if they are to survive, are forced, at last, to tell the whole story, to vomit the anguish up."

BALDWIN: Art has to be a kind of confession. I don't mean a true confession in the sense of that dreary magazine. The effort, it seems to me, is: if you can examine and face your life, you can discover the terms with which you are connected to other lives, and they can discover, too, the terms with which they are connected to other people.

This has happened to every one of us, I'm sure. You read something which you thought only happened to you, and you discovered it happened one hundred years ago to Dostoyevsky. This is a very great liberation for the suffering, struggling person, who always thinks that he is alone. This is why art is important. Art would not be important if life were not important, and life *is* important.

Most of us, no matter what we say, are walking in the dark, whistling in the dark. Nobody knows what is going to happen to him from one moment to the next, or how one will bear it. This is irreducible. And it's true for everybody. Now, it is true that the nature of society is to create, among its citizens, an illusion of safety; but it is also absolutely true that the safety is always necessarily an illusion. Artists are here to disturb the peace.

TERKEL: Artists are here to disturb the peace?

BALDWIN: Yes, they have to disturb the peace. Otherwise, chaos.

TERKEL: Life is risk.

BALDWIN: It is, indeed. It always is. People have to know this. In some way they will have to know it in order to get through their risks.

TERKEL: So the safety itself is wholly illusory?

BALDWIN: There's no such thing as safety on this planet. No one *knows* that much. No one ever will. Not only about the world but about himself. That's why it's unsafe.

This is what the whole sense of tragedy is really about. People think that a sense of tragedy is a kind of . . . embroidery, something irrelevant, that you can take or leave. But, in fact, it is a necessity. That's what the Blues and Spirituals are all about. It is the ability to look on things as they are and survive your losses, or even not survive them—to know that your losses are coming. To know they are coming is the only possible insurance you have, a faint insurance, that you will survive them.

TERKEL: Again, in your book, you mention that Americans, although we have tremendous potentialities, are lacking in that which non-Americans may have: a sense of tragedy.

BALDWIN: It's incredible to me that—and I'm not trying to oversimplify anything—in this country where, after all, one is for the most part better off materially than anywhere else in the world: it is incredible that one should know so many people who are in a state of the most absolute insecurity about themselves. They literally can't get through a morning without going to see the psychiatrist. I find it very difficult to take this really seriously.

Other people who have really terrifying and unimaginable troubles, from the American point of view, don't dream of going anywhere near a psychiatrist, and wouldn't do it even if they were mad enough to dream of it. This seems a very great, well, not illness, exactly, but fear. Frenchmen and Frenchwomen whom I knew spent much less time in this dreadful and internal warfare, tearing themselves and each other to pieces, than Americans do.

Why this is so is probably a question for someone else; but it *is* so, and I think it says something serious about the real aim and the real standards of our society. People don't live by the standards they say they live by, and the gap between their profession and the actuality is what creates this despair, and this uncertainty, which is very, very dangerous.

TERKEL: In your essay "The Black Boy Looks at the White Boy," you explore your relationship with Norman Mailer. You infer that the White Boy, if he can deal as truthfully as he knows how with our present fortunes, these present days, these "sad and stormy events," and if he has understood them, "then he is richer and we are richer, too; if he has not understood them, we are all much poorer. For, though it clearly needs to be brought into focus, he has a real vision of ourselves as we are, and it cannot be too often repeated in this country now, that, where there is no vision, the people perish."

BALDWIN: I mean that.

TERKEL: During this hour, which has passed so ludicrously fast, we have only scratched the surface in getting to know James Baldwin, who has confessed in a very beautiful way. Besides *Nobody Knows My Name*, he has written two earlier novels, *Giovanni's Room* and *Go Tell It on the Mountain*, and now, the forthcoming novel . . .

BALDWIN: *Another Country*. It is about this country.

TERKEL: One last question. James Baldwin: who are you, now?

BALDWIN: [*Long pause*] Who, indeed. Well, I may be able to tell you who I am, but I am also discovering who I am not. I want to be an honest man. And I want to be a good writer. I don't know if one ever gets to be what one wants to be. You just have to play it by ear, and . . . pray for rain.

JAMES BALDWIN— REFLECTIONS OF A MAVERICK

INTERVIEW BY JULIUS LESTER
THE NEW YORK TIMES BOOK REVIEW
MAY 27, 1984

The hair is almost white now, but that is the only indication that James Baldwin will be sixty years old in August. Thirty-one years have passed since the publication of his first book, the novel *Go Tell It on the Mountain*, and twenty-one years since *The Fire Next Time* made him an international celebrity.

The intensity and passion that characterize his writing are evident in conversation. His voice, though soft, is deep and resonant, and in its modulations and rhythms one hears echoes of the boy preacher he once was. He gestures with a fluidity reminiscent of a conductor, as if there is an unseen orchestra that must be brought into harmony. The face he has written of as ugly, with its protuberant eyes, flat nose and wide mouth, has, in reality, the ritual beauty of a Benin head. Baldwin looks as if he were sculpted in flesh rather than merely being born of it.

The following is the edited transcript of a three-hour conversation taped in my home in Amherst, Massachusetts, on a Sunday afternoon in April. As writers, fifteen years apart in age, we wanted to compare our generations. As it turned out, we embodied our generations more than I, at least, had anticipated.

LESTER: Your literary beginnings were as a part of the New York intelligentsia. It was right after the end of World War II that you began publishing reviews and essays in publications like *The New Leader*, *The Nation*, *Commentary* and *Partisan Review*. What was it like for a young black man, twenty-one years old, to be around people like Randall Jarrell, Dwight Macdonald, Lionel Trilling, Delmore Schwartz, Irving Howe and William Barrett, to name a few?

BALDWIN: For me, these people were kind of an Olympus. I mean, in one way I was very intimidated by them, and I don't know what in the world they thought of me. Dwight Macdonald told me that I was "terribly smart." [*Laughs*] I certainly learned from them, though I could not tell you exactly what I learned. A certain confidence in myself, perhaps.

LESTER: Did you ever approach Langston Hughes? He was living in Harlem.

BALDWIN: I knew of Langston Hughes, but it never occurred to me. I was too shy. Later on I realized that I could have. He didn't live far away, but it wouldn't have occurred to me. You see, there were two Harlems. These were those who lived in Sugar Hill and there was the Hollow, where we lived. There was a great divide between the black people on the Hill and

39

us. I was just a ragged, funky black shoeshine boy and was afraid of the people on the Hill, who, for their part, didn't want to have anything to do with me. Langston, in fact, did not live on the Hill, but in my mind, he was associated with those people. So I would never have dreamed of going and knocking on his door.

LESTER: And yet, you went and knocked on Richard Wright's door.

BALDWIN: I suppose I did that because I had to. I'd just read *Uncle Tom's Children* and *Native Son*. I knew of Langston and Countee Cullen, they were the only other black writers whose work I knew at that time, but for some reason they did not attract me. I'm not putting them down, but the world they were describing had nothing to do with me, at that time in my life. Later on I realized something else, but then their work did not resound to me. The black middle class was essentially an abstraction to me. Richard was very different, though. The life he described was the life I lived. I recognized the tenements. I knew that rat in *Native Son*. I knew that woman in the story "Bright and Morning Star." All of that was urgent for me. And it was through Richard that I came to read the black writers who had preceded me, like Jean Toomer, and came to know Langston and Countee Cullen in a new way. By the time I went to see Richard I was committed to the idea of being a writer, though I knew how impossible it was. Maybe I went to see Richard to see if he would laugh at me.

LESTER: Did he?

BALDWIN: No. He was very nice to me. I think he found me kind of amusing and I'm sure I was. He was very distant in a way—we never got to be close friends. But he was very tender, very helpful and we saw each other from time to time. I was still very shy, but I was very proud of him and I think he was proud of me . . . for a while. He may have been always, in fact.

LESTER: In the essay "Alas, Poor Richard" you write about Wright's feeling that in your earlier essays, "Many Thousands Gone" and "Everybody's Protest Novel," you were trying to kill him—

BALDWIN: That I betrayed him.

LESTER: —And, I think, then, about Eldridge Cleaver's essay "Notes on a Native Son" from *Soul on Ice*, which is critical of you. Have younger black writers looked on you as the literary father who must be killed?

BALDWIN: I've never bought that analogy. Eldridge's attack on me—quite apart from everything else—is preposterous. In any case, Eldridge cannot claim to know me in any way whatsoever. And he certainly didn't love me. I knew Richard and I loved him. And that's a very, very, very great difference. I was not attacking him; I was trying to clarify something for myself. The analogy does not hold. I reject it in toto.

LESTER: It is clear that you were trying to clarify something in yourself, but you certainly were very critical of him. And I can certainly understand how he could've reacted as he did.

BALDWIN: But what are the reasons for that? I thought—and I still think—that a lot of what happened to us in Paris occurred because Richard was much, much better than a lot of the company he kept. I mean, the French existentialists. I didn't think that Simone de Beauvoir or Jean-Paul Sartre—to say nothing of the American colony—had any right whatsover to patronize that man. It revolted me and made me furious. And it made me furious at Richard, too, because he was better than that. A lot of my tone [in the essay] comes out of that . . . Alas, poor Richard.

LESTER: Did he have a responsibility for you as a younger black writer, and do you have a responsibility for younger black writers?

BALDWIN: No, no. I never felt that Richard had a responsibility for me, and if he had, he'd discharged it. What I was thinking about, though, was the early 1950's when the world of white supremacy was breaking up. I'm talking about the revolutions all over the world. Specifically, since we were in Paris, those in Tunisia, Algeria, the ferment in Senegal, the French loss of their Indo-Chinese empire. A whole lot of people—darker people, for the most part—came from all kinds of places to Richard's door as they do now to my door. And in that sense, he had a responsibility that he didn't know—well, who can blame him?

LESTER: This may be one of those generational differences, but I don't know that I understand this claim you say black people have on you.

BALDWIN: I see what you're saying. But it's not only black people, if you like. There is something unjust in it, but it's an irreducible injustice, I think. I found no way around it. But you can't execute the responsibility in the way people want you to. You have to do your work. But, at the same time, you're out there. You asked for it. And no matter how you react to it, you cannot pretend that it is not happening.

LESTER: Do you ever resent the claim?

BALDWIN: It has given me some trying moments, but "It comes with the territory." It is not my fault and it is not their fault that the world thinks it's white. Therefore someone who is not white and attempts to be in some way responsible is going to be claimed by multitudes of black kids. Just or unjust is irrelevant.

LESTER: "Witness" is a word I've heard you use often to describe yourself. It is not a word I would apply to myself as a writer, and I don't know if any black writers with whom I am contemporary would, or even could, use the word. What are you a witness to?

BALDWIN: Witness to whence I came, where I am. Witness to what I've seen and the possibilities that I think I see ... But I can see what you're saying. I don't think I ever resented it, but it exhausted me. I didn't resent it because it was an obligation that was impossible to fulfill. They have made you, produced you—and they have done so precisely so they could claim you. They can treat you very badly sometimes, as has happened to me. Still, they produced you because they need you and, for me, there's no way around that. Now, in order for me to execute what I see as my responsibility, I may have to offend them all, but that also comes with the territory. I don't see how I can repudiate it. I'm not trying to suggest, by the way, that Richard tried to repudiate it, either.

LESTER: You have been politically engaged, but you have never succumbed to ideology, which has devoured some of the best black writers of my generation.

BALDWIN: Perhaps I did not succumb to ideology, as you put it, because I have never seen myself as a spokesman. I am a witness. In the church in which I was raised you were supposed to bear witness to the truth. Now, later on, you wonder what in the world the truth is, but you do know what a lie is.

LESTER: What's the difference between a spokesman and a witness?

BALDWIN: A spokesman assumes that he is speaking for others. I never assumed that—I never assumed that I could. Fannie Lou Hamer [the Mississippi civil rights organizer], for example, could speak very eloquently for herself. What I tried to do, or to interpret and make clear was that what the Republic was doing to that woman, it was also doing to itself. No society can smash the social contract and be exempt from the consequences, and the consequences are chaos for everybody in the society.

LESTER: There's a confidence in your use of the word "witness"—a confidence about the way the world is and the way it should be. I wonder if it's possible for writers now, black or white, to have that confidence. I wonder if the world hasn't changed between the time you started and the time we started.

BALDWIN: Well, it may have. In one way or another, one is very much a prisoner of his time. But I know what I've seen and what I've seen makes me know I have to say, *I know.* I won't say I believe, because I know that we can be better than we are. That's the sum total of my wisdom in all these years. We can also be infinitely worse, but I know that the world we live in now is not necessarily the best world we can make. I can't be entirely wrong. There're two things we have to do— love each other and raise our children. We have to do that! The alternative, for me, would be suicide.

LESTER: That sounds romantic to me.

BALDWIN: I don't think I'm romantic. If I am, I wouldn't know it, so it's kind of a fruitless question.

LESTER: When you say that the two things we have to do are love each other and raise our children, my response is to look at American society and say we don't do either very well.

BALDWIN: That's quite true. But the fact that American society doesn't do that doesn't get us off the hook. In fact, black people have attempted to do that.

LESTER: Have they? The first thing I think of is the black men selling junk to black children.

BALDWIN: I know that very well. I think I know why in any case, and I'm not claiming that black people are better than white people. We treat each other just the way the rest of the human race treats itself. Abominably. Well, what am I to do in the face of that? The black man selling junk to kids, I'd like to kill him. I don't think I'm romantic about that. But I do know, too, that some of the evils that we live with are really produced by the society we live in, by the choices that society offers. I'm not trying to get anybody off the hook when I say that.

LESTER: It sounds like it.

BALDWIN: No, I don't think so. For example, going back to the years in Greenwich Village, the years I was getting my head beaten when I was walking the streets, that doesn't happen now. Or it happens more rarely, or in a different way. This means that the choice that a white person had to make when I was growing up—to be seen or not be seen with me, to be on my side or not to be on my side—that choice is a little less dangerous now. That infinitesimal change makes things a little easier for everybody.

LESTER: Are there any white writers you would describe as witnesses?

BALDWIN: Dostoyevsky, Dickens, James, Proust.

LESTER: What about of your generation?

BALDWIN: Well, bearing in mind that this is for the *New York Times*, whatever I say I'm in a trick bag. Whomever I name, there'll be a lot of people I'll have left out. I won't have a friend left. The only way I can answer the question would be to say that, generally, most white American writers think of themselves as white. To be a white American is to have a very peculiar inheritance. All white American writers came from someplace else, even if they were born here. My past, after all, stretches back to Africa by way of Europe. But most white American writers seem to have cut off their heritage at Ellis Island. Their testimony, for me, does not include enough. Or, one could put it another way. One could say that they reveal their heritage in unconscious ways. I could say this about Norman Mailer, for example. I think, for example, of John Updike and John Cheever, whose subject matter is roughly the same. But Cheever brought something to that subject that engages me—while John Updike's people do not engage me.

LESTER: What do you think Cheever brought to his work?

BALDWIN: Perhaps a depth of anguish. Somehow those lost suburbanites in Cheever's fiction are very moving. He engages your compassion. His people are not remote. The work of so many white writers is remote for me. I'm not trying to put them down. It's simply that they are not relevant to my experience. My experience is larger, and my comment says more about me than them. I think, too, that the effort on the part of the Republic to avoid the presence of black people reflects itself in American literature fatally, to the detriment of that literature.

LESTER: What about somebody like William Styron?

BALDWIN: Bill? Bill is a kind of exception, if only in the effort. I'm thinking, of course, of his *Confessions of Nat Turner*, which has been so violently attacked and so praised and over-praised. It's a book I admire very much. But, you see, I read that book as the *Confessions of Bill Styron*—and I'm not trying to put the book down when I say that. I respect the book very much. I respect him very much and I respect his attempt to grapple with something almost no one in his generation is prepared to even look at.

LESTER: I was curious about that, because when the book came out, you were the only black writer, as I recall, who liked it, and I felt a large generational gap between you and me.

BALDWIN: I think that I was right.

LESTER: Well, I have to question that. Perhaps my profound dissatisfaction with *The Confessions of Nat Turner* comes from my sense of its inadequate execution, as well as my wish that he had written it from the point of view of a white person affected by the Turner uprising. If he'd done that I could agree with you that he was attempting to grapple with something.

BALDWIN: I can understand the objection you're raising, but I think it's finally irrelevant. I think Bill wrote the book from that point of view because he couldn't find another one, he had to try to put himself in the skin of Nat Turner. Now that may have been a great error, but I can't condemn him for it. It's beyond my province, really. The book meant something to me because it was a white Southern writer's attempt to deal with something that was tormenting him and frightening him. I respect him very much for that. Now, as to his execution, what is one to say about it?

LESTER: I'm still waiting for the white writer to write a novel about a lynching from the point of view of the lyncher.

BALDWIN: Yes, I quite agree with you. I said before that America's effort to avoid the presence of black people constricts American literature. It creates a trap white writers find themselves in.

LESTER: We were talking about white writers as witnesses and you alluded to Mailer. How do you see Mailer?

BALDWIN: Well, Mailer is something I've been desperately trying to avoid. [*Laughs*] All I can say is that—well, one of the hazards of being an American writer, and I'm well placed to know it, is that eventually you have nothing to write about. A funny thing happens on the way to the typewriter. There is a decidedly grave danger of becoming a celebrity, of becoming a star, of becoming a personality. Again, I'm very well placed to know that. It's symptomatic of the society that doesn't have any real respect for the artist. You're either a success or a failure and there's nothing in between. And if you are a success, you run the risk that Norman has run and that I run, too, of becoming a kind of show business personality. Then the legend becomes far more important than the work. It's as though you're living in an echo chamber. You hear only your own voice. And, when you become a celebrity, that voice is magnified by multitudes and you begin to drown in this endless duplication of what looks like yourself. You have to be really very lucky, and very stubborn, not to let that happen to you. It's a difficult trap to avoid. And that's part of Norman's dilemma, I think. A writer is supposed to write. If he appears on television or as a public speaker, so much the better or so much the worse, but the public persona is one thing. On the public platform or on television. I have to sound as if I know what I'm talking about. It's antithetical to the effort you make at the typewriter, where you don't know a damned thing. And you have to know you don't know it. The moment you carry the persona to the typewriter, you are finished. Does that answer your question?

LESTER: No, but it's an eloquent evasion.

BALDWIN: Is it? But I don't want to talk about Norman! Why should I talk about Norman? I'm very fond of him and have great respect for his gifts. Well, perhaps he's a perfect example of what it means to be a white writer in this century, a white American writer in this country. It affords too many opportunities to avoid reality ... And I know much more about Norman than I'm willing to say in print. After all, I care about him.

LESTER: I respect that, but I'd like to pursue it from another angle.

BALDWIN: I'll have another drink, then.

LESTER: In "Alas, Poor Richard," you write that it's "not possible to overstate the price a Negro pays to climb out of obscurity." And you go on to write that "The higher he rises, the less is his journey worth." Thinking about what you've just said about Mailer, I couldn't help also thinking that you've risen higher than any black writer, even higher than Wright in terms of public acclaim, recognition and esteem. How much has the journey been worth?

BALDWIN: What happened to me came as a great surprise. Obviously, in the essay, I'm speaking to some extent of a public journey, though the word "public" is not used. I don't feel bitter about the journey, and that may be indicative of something. I don't feel bitter and I don't feel betrayed. I was a maverick, a maverick in the sense that I depended on neither the white world nor the black world. That was the only way I could've played it. I would've been broken otherwise. I had to say, "A curse on both your houses." The fact that I went to Europe so early is probably what saved me. It gave me another touchstone—myself. Then the idea of becoming an artist as distinguished from a celebrity was real. I never wanted to become a celebrity. Being a maverick saved my life. What club could I have joined? I had to make peace with a great many things, not the least of which was my intelligence. You don't realize that you're intelligent until it gets you into trouble.

LESTER: Is the celebrity James Baldwin anyone that you know?

BALDWIN: That's a very good question. Not really. Not really. It's almost a garment I wear. But the celebrity never sees himself. I have some idea what I'm doing on that stage; above all, I have some idea what sustains me on that stage. But the celebrity is not exactly Jimmy, though he comes out of Jimmy and Jimmy nourishes that, too. I can see now, with hindsight, that I would've had to become a celebrity in order to survive. A boy like me with all his handicaps, real and fancied, could not have survived in obscurity. I can say that it would have had to happen this way, though I could not see it coming.

LESTER: One night you were talking semicoherently about facing the fact of having to find a new language.

BALDWIN: Where was I? Oh, yes! I was here—at least I wasn't on television. Anyway, a language is a frame of reference, isn't it? And I can only be semicoherent about it now because I'm in the process of experimenting. I say a new language. I might say a new morality, which, in my terms, comes to the same thing. And that's on all levels—the level of color, the level of identity, the level of sexual identity, what love means, especially in a consumer society, for example. Everything is in question, according to me. One has to forge a new language to deal with it. That's as coherent as I can be about it.

LESTER: What do you see as the task facing black writers today, regardless of age or generation?

BALDWIN: This may sound strange, but I would say to make the question of color obsolete.

LESTER: And how would a black writer do that?

BALDWIN: Well, you ask me a reckless question, I'll give you a reckless answer—by realizing first of all that the world is not white. And by realizing that the real terror that engulfs the white world now is a visceral terror. I can't prove this, but I know it. It's the terror of being described by those they've been describing for so long. And that will make the concept of color obsolete. Do you see what I mean?

LESTER: I see what you mean, but some black writers of my generation might say that the responsibility of black writers is to write about black people.

BALDWIN: That is not a contradiction. If our voices are heard, it makes the concept of color obsolete. That has to be its inevitable result.

"GO THE WAY YOUR BLOOD BEATS"
AN INTERVIEW WITH JAMES BALDWIN

INTERVIEW BY RICHARD GOLDSTEIN
THE VILLAGE VOICE
JUNE 26, 1984

In the early 1980s I read a long interview with James Baldwin in *The New York Times Book Review*, which didn't include a whisper about its subject's sexuality. Since I belong to the generation of gay men for whom Baldwin's fiction was an early vector of self-discovery, I decided to broach the subject for myself. So I tracked Baldwin down and badgered him with politics and personal charm until he agreed to meet me at the Riviera Café in the Village, an old hangout for him. When I arrived, Baldwin was sitting at an outside table, watching the exotica with that faintly distracted look Europeans cultivate. I proceeded to "orient" him for the interview that would follow, only to discover that he knew very little about the state of American gay life today: What's a "clone," he wanted to know, and how is AIDS transmitted? What transpired over the next few days was one of the most powerful experiences of my professional life—an insight into the paradoxical nature of gay culture from a man who traced much of his acuity and pain to the nexus of racism and homophobia. But what I remember most about that afternoon is the sight of Baldwin, gnomelike and far from serene, surrounded by passersby who recognize him, and just wanted to say, as I did, how full of him our lives will always be.

GOLDSTEIN: Do you feel like a stranger in gay America?

BALDWIN: Well, first of all I feel like a stranger in America from almost every conceivable angle except, oddly enough, as a black person. The word "gay" has always rubbed me the wrong way. I never understood exactly what is meant by it. I don't want to sound distant or patronizing because I don't really feel that. I simply feel it's a world that has very little to do with me, with where I did my growing up. I was never at home in it. Even in my early years in the Village, what I saw of that world absolutely frightened me, bewildered me. I didn't understand the necessity of all the role playing. And in a way I still don't.

GOLDSTEIN: You never thought of yourself as being gay?

BALDWIN: No. I didn't have a word for it. The only one I had was "homosexual" and that didn't quite cover whatever it was I was beginning to feel. Even when I began to realize things about myself, began to suspect who I was and what I was likely to become, it was still very personal, absolutely personal. It was really a matter between me and God. I would have to live the life he had made me to live. I told him quite a long, long time ago there would be two of us at the Mercy Seat. He would not be asking all the questions.

GOLDSTEIN: When did you first begin to think of yourself in those terms?

BALDWIN: It hit me with great force while I was in the pulpit. I must have been fourteen. I was still a virgin. I had no idea what you were supposed to do about it. I didn't really understand any of what I felt except I knew I loved one boy, for example. But it was private. And by the time I left home, when I was seventeen or eighteen and still a virgin, it was like everything else in my life, a problem which I would have to resolve myself. You know, it never occurred to me to join a club. I must say I felt very, very much alone. But I was alone on so many levels and this was one more aspect of it.

GOLDSTEIN: So when we talk about gay life, which is so group-oriented, so tribal . . .

BALDWIN: And I am not that kind of person at all.

GOLDSTEIN: . . . do you feel baffled by it?

BALDWIN: I feel remote from it. It's a phenomenon that came along much after I was formed. In some sense, I couldn't have afforded it. You see, I am not a member of anything. I joined the Church when I was very, very young, and haven't joined anything since, except for a brief stint in the Socialist Party. I'm a maverick, you know. But that doesn't mean I don't feel very strongly for my brothers and sisters.

GOLDSTEIN: Do you have a special feeling of responsibility toward gay people?

BALDWIN: Toward that phenomenon we call gay, yeah. I feel special responsibility because I would have to be a kind of witness to it, you know.

GOLDSTEIN: You're one of the architects of it by the act of writing about it publicly and elevating it into the realm of literature.

BALDWIN: I made a public announcement that we're private, if you see what I mean.

GOLDSTEIN: When I consider what a risk it must have been to write about homosexuality when you did . . .

BALDWIN: You're talking about *Giovanni's Room*. Yeah, that was rough. But I had to do it to clarify something for myself.

GOLDSTEIN: What was that?

BALDWIN: Where I was in the world. I mean, what I'm made of. Anyway, *Giovanni's Room* is not really about homosexuality. It's the vehicle through which the book moves. *Go Tell It on the Mountain*, for example, is not about a church, and *Giovanni* is not really about homosexuality. It's about what happens to you if you're afraid to love anybody. Which is much more interesting than the question of homosexuality.

GOLDSTEIN: But you didn't mask the sexuality.

BALDWIN: No.

GOLDSTEIN: And that decision alone must have been enormously risky.

BALDWIN: Yeah. The alternative was worse.

GOLDSTEIN: What would that have been?

BALDWIN: If I hadn't written that book I would probably have had to stop writing altogether.

GOLDSTEIN: It was that serious.

BALDWIN: It *is* that serious. The question of human affection, of integrity, in my case, the question of trying to become a writer, are all linked with the question of sexuality. Sexuality is only a part of it. I don't know even if it's the most important part. But it's indispensable.

GOLDSTEIN: Did people advise you not to write the book so candidly?

BALDWIN: I didn't ask anybody. When I turned the book in, I was told I shouldn't have written it. I was told to bear in mind that I was a young Negro writer with a certain audience, and I wasn't supposed to alienate that audience. And if I published the book, it would wreck my career. They wouldn't publish the book, they said, as a favor to me. So I took the book to England and I sold it there before I sold it here.

GOLDSTEIN: Do you think your unresolved sexuality motivated you, at the start, to write?

BALDWIN: Yeah. Well, everything was unresolved. The sexual thing was only one of the things. It was for a while the most tormenting thing and it could have been the most dangerous.

GOLDSTEIN: How so?

BALDWIN: Well, because it frightened me so much.

GOLDSTEIN: I don't think straight people realize how frightening it is to finally admit to yourself that this is going to be you forever.

BALDWIN: It's very frightening. But the so-called straight person is no safer than I am really. Loving anybody and being loved by anybody is a tremendous danger, a tremendous responsibility. Loving of children, raising of children. The terrors homosexuals go through in this society would not be so great if the society itself did not go through so many terrors which it doesn't want to admit. The discovery of one's sexual preference doesn't have to be a trauma. It's a trauma because it's such a traumatized society.

GOLDSTEIN: Have you got any sense of what causes people to hate homosexuals?

BALDWIN: Terror, I suppose. Terror of the flesh. After all, we're supposed to mortify the flesh, a doctrine which has led to untold horrors. This is a very biblical culture; people believe the wages of sin is death. In fact, the wages of sin *is* death, but not the way the moral guardians of this time and place understand it.

GOLDSTEIN: Is there a particularly American component of homophobia?

BALDWIN: I think Americans are terrified of feeling anything. And homophobia is simply an extreme example of the American terror that's concerned with growing up. I never met a people more infantile in my life.

GOLDSTEIN: You sound like Leslie Fiedler.

BALDWIN: I hope not. [*Laughter*]

GOLDSTEIN: Are you as apocalyptic about the prospects for sexual reconciliation as you are about racial reconciliation?

BALDWIN: Well, they join. The sexual question and the racial question have always been entwined, you know. If Americans can mature on the level of racism, then they have to mature on the level of sexuality.

GOLDSTEIN: I think we would agree there's a retrenchment going on in race relations. Do you sense that happening also in sex relations?

BALDWIN: Yeah. There's what we would have to call a backlash which, I'm afraid, is just beginning.

GOLDSTEIN: I suspect most gay people have fantasies about genocide.

BALDWIN: Well, it's not a fantasy exactly since the society makes its will toward you very, very clear. Especially the police, for example, or truck drivers. I know from my own experience that the macho men—truck drivers, cops, football players—these people are far more complex than they want to realize. That's why I call them infantile. They have needs which, for them, are literally inexpressible. They don't dare look into the mirror. And that is why they need faggots. They've created faggots in order to act out a sexual fantasy on the body of another man and not take any responsibility for it. Do you see what I mean? I think it's very important for the male homosexual to recognize that he is a sexual target for other men, and that is why he is despised, and why he is called a faggot. He is called a faggot because other males need him.

GOLDSTEIN: Why do you think homophobia falls so often on the right of the political spectrum?

BALDWIN: It's a way of controlling people. Nobody really cares who goes to bed with whom, finally. I mean, the State doesn't really care, the Church doesn't really care. They care that you should be frightened of what you do. As long as you feel guilty about it, the State can rule you. It's a way of exerting control over the universe, by terrifying people.

GOLDSTEIN: Why don't black ministers need to share in this rhetoric?

BALDWIN: Perhaps because they're more grown-up than most white ministers.

GOLDSTEIN: Did you never hear antigay rhetoric in church?

BALDWIN: Not in the church I grew up in. I'm sure that's still true. Everyone is a child of God, according to us.

GOLDSTEIN: Didn't people ever call you "faggot" uptown?

BALDWIN: Of course. But there's a difference in the way it's used. It's got less venom, at least in my experience. I don't know of anyone who has ever denied his brother or his sister because they were gay. No doubt it happens. It must happen. But in the generality, a black person has got quite a lot to get through the day without getting entangled in all the American fantasies.

GOLDSTEIN: Do black gay people have the same sense of being separate as white gay people do? I mean, I feel distinct from other white people.

BALDWIN: Well, that I think is because you are penalized, as it were, unjustly; you're placed outside a certain safety to which you think you were born. A black gay person who is a sexual conundrum to society is already, long before the question of sexuality comes into it, menaced and marked because he's black or she's black. The sexual question comes after the question of color; it's simply one more aspect of the danger in which all black people live. I think white gay people feel cheated because they were born, in principle, into a society in which they were supposed to be safe. The anomaly of their sexuality puts them in danger, unexpectedly. Their reaction seems to me in direct proportion to the sense of feeling cheated of the advantages which accrue to white people in a white society. There's an element, it has always seemed to me, of bewilderment and complaint. Now that may sound very harsh, but the gay world as such is no more prepared to accept black people than anywhere else in society. It's a very hermetically sealed world with very unattractive features, including racism.

GOLDSTEIN: Are you optimistic about the possibilities of blacks and gays forging a political coalition? Do you see any special basis for empathy between us?

BALDWIN: Yeah. Of course.

GOLDSTEIN: What would that be?

BALDWIN: Well, the basis would be shared suffering, shared perceptions, shared hopes.

GOLDSTEIN: What perceptions do we share?

BALDWIN: I supposed one would be the perception that love is where you find it. If you see what I mean.

GOLDSTEIN: [*Laughter*] Or where you lose it, for that matter.

BALDWIN: Uhm-hmm.

GOLDSTEIN: But are gay people sensitized by the perceptions we share with blacks?

BALDWIN: Not in my experience, no.

GOLDSTEIN: So I guess you're not very hopeful about that kind of coalition as something that could make a difference in urban politics.

BALDWIN: It's simply that the whole question has entered my mind another way. I know a great many white people, men and women, straight and gay, whatever, who are unlike the majority of their countrymen. On what basis we could form a coalition is still an open question. The idea of basing it on sexual preference strikes me as somewhat dubious, strikes me as being less than a firm foundation. It seems to me that a coalition has to be based on the grounds of human dignity. Anyway, what connects us, speaking about the private life, is mainly unspoken.

GOLDSTEIN: I sometimes think gay people look to black people as healing them . . .

BALDWIN: Not only gay people.

GOLDSTEIN: . . . healing their alienation.

BALDWIN: That has to be done, first of all, by the person and then you will find your company.

GOLDSTEIN: When I heard Jesse Jackson speak before a gay audience, I wanted him to say there wasn't any sin, that I was forgiven.

BALDWIN: Is that a question for you still? That question of sin?

GOLDSTEIN: I think it must be, on some level, even though I am not a believer.

BALDWIN: How peculiar. I didn't realize you thought of it as sin. Do many gay people feel that?

GOLDSTEIN: I don't know. [*Laughter*] I guess I'm throwing something at you, which is the idea that gays look to blacks as conferring a kind of acceptance by embracing them in a coalition. I find it unavoidable to think in those terms. When I fantasize about a black mayor or a black president, I think of it as being better for gay people.

BALDWIN: Well, don't be romantic about black people. Though I can see what you mean.

GOLDSTEIN: Do you think black people have heightened capacity for tolerance, even acceptance, in its truest sense?

BALDWIN: Well, there is a capacity in black people for

experience, simply. And that capacity makes other things possible. It dictates the depth of one's acceptance of other people. The capacity for experience is what burns out fear. Because the homophobia we're talking about really is a kind of fear. It's a terror of flesh. It's really a terror of being able to be touched.

GOLDSTEIN: Do you think about having children?

BALDWIN: Not anymore. It's one thing I really regret, maybe the only regret I have. But I couldn't have managed it then. Now it's too late.

GOLDSTEIN: But you're not disturbed by the idea of gay men being parents.

BALDWIN: Look, men have been sleeping with men for thousands of years—and raising tribes. This is a Western sickness, it really is. It's an artificial division. Men will be sleeping with each other when the trumpet sounds. It's only this infantile culture which has made such a big deal of it.

GOLDSTEIN: So you think of homosexuality as universal?

BALDWIN: Of course. There's nothing in me that is not in everybody else, and nothing in everybody else that is not in me. We're trapped in language, of course. But "homosexual" is not a noun. At least not in my book.

GOLDSTEIN: What part of speech would it be?

BALDWIN: Perhaps a verb. You see, I can only talk about my own life. I loved a few people and they loved me. It had nothing to do with these labels. Of course, the world has all kinds of words for us. But that's the world's problem.

GOLDSTEIN: Is it problematic for you, the idea of having sex only with other people who are identified as gay?

BALDWIN: Well, you see, my life has not been like that at all. The people who were my lovers were never, well, the word "gay" wouldn't have meant anything to them.

GOLDSTEIN: That means that they moved in the straight world.

BALDWIN: They moved in the world.

GOLDSTEIN: Do you think of the gay world as being a false refuge?

BALDWIN: I think perhaps it imposes a limitation which is unnecessary. It seems to me simply a man is a man, a woman is a woman, and who they go to bed with is nobody's business but theirs. I suppose what I am really saying is that one's sexual preference is a private matter. I resent the interference of the State, or the Church, or any institution in my only journey to whatever it is we are journeying toward. But it has been made a public question by the institutions of this country. I can see how the gay world comes about in response to that. And to contradict myself, I suppose, or more precisely, I hope that it is easier for the transgressor to become reconciled with himself or herself than it was for many people in my generation—and it was difficult for me. It is difficult to be despised, in short. And if the so-called gay movement can cause men and women, boys and girls, to come to some kind of terms with themselves more speedily and with less pain, then that's a very great advance. I'm not sure it can be done on that level. My own point of view, speaking out of black America, when I had to try to answer that stigma, that species of social curse, it seemed a great mistake to answer in the language of the oppressor. As long as I react as a "nigger," as long as I protest my case on evidence or assumptions held by others, I'm simply reinforcing those assumptions. As long as I complain about being oppressed, the oppressor is in consolation of knowing that I know my place, so to speak.

GOLDSTEIN: You will always come forward and make the statement that you're homosexual. You will never hide it, or deny it. And yet you refuse to make a life out of it?

BALDWIN: Yeah. That sums it up pretty well.

GOLDSTEIN: That strikes me as a balance some of us might want to look to, in a climate where it's possible.

BALDWIN: One has to make that climate for oneself.

GOLDSTEIN: Do you have good fantasies about the future?

BALDWIN: I have good fantasies and bad fantasies.

GOLDSTEIN: What are some of the good ones?

BALDWIN: Oh, that I am working toward the New Jerusalem. That's true, I'm not joking. I won't live to see it but I do believe in it. I think we're going to be better than we are.

GOLDSTEIN: What do you think gay people will be like then?

BALDWIN: No one will have to call themselves gay. Maybe that's at the bottom of my impatience with the term. It answers a false argument, a false accusation.

GOLDSTEIN: Which is what?

BALDWIN: Which is that you have no right to be here, that you have to prove your right to be here. I'm saying I have nothing to prove. The world also belongs to me.

GOLDSTEIN: What advice would you give a gay man who's about to come out?

BALDWIN: Coming out means to publicly say?

GOLDSTEIN: I guess I'm imposing these terms on you.

BALDWIN: Yeah, they're not my terms. But what advice can you possibly give? Best advice I ever got was an old friend of mine, a black friend, who said you have to go the way your blood beats. If you don't live the only life you have, you won't live some other life, you won't live any life at all. That's the only advice you can give anybody. And it's not advice, it's an observation.

THE LAST
INTERVIEW

INTEVIEW BY QUINCY TROUPE
ST. PAUL DE VENCE, FRANCE
NOVEMBER 1987

On November 13, 1987, I flew from Paris to Nice to visit the distinguished American writer James Baldwin. Jimmy was an old friend who quite generously and without fail had always been there with his encouragement and help throughout my writing career. He always extended an invitation to me to visit him whenever I had the time, and I wanted to interview him for the Miles Davis autobiography I was writing with Davis. I also had heard that Jimmy was quite ill, and I wanted an opportunity to see him again.

On that gray morning I thought of James Baldwin and of the writer Richard Wright, among others, who would never be honored in the United States, as they were abroad, simply because they were Black. On the flight down to Nice, this thought profoundly saddened and troubled me. But by the time I arrived at Nice's Côte d'Azur airport, my spirits had lifted considerably, no doubt due in large measure to the sun-splashed beauty of Nice, but also because David Baldwin, Jimmy's brother, was there at the airport to greet me.

After I had collected my bags, on the way out of the airport, David informed me quite matter-of-factly that Jimmy had cancer and that the prognosis was that it was terminal. "At the most," he said, "the doctor gives him about a month." I was stunned, knocked off balance by the finality of the news and also by David's casual manner. But he added that he and others close by had decided to have an upbeat attitude about everything so that Jimmy's last days could be as normal as possible. David also told me that Jimmy had not been told that his cancer was terminal, although he believed that Jimmy probably knew because of the rapid deterioration of his physical condition. He said he was telling me this to prepare me for the way Jimmy looked. As he went on in more detail I could see the unspeakable grief etched in the mask that was now his face.

On the winding drive up the mountain to Venice, David asked me to conduct an in-depth interview with Jimmy. Because of Jimmy's rapidly deteriorating condition, David knew that this would be the last opportunity for Jimmy to air his final thoughts and observations. Although that was what I hoped to do, I hadn't really expected the situation to be as grave as it was.

Just down the hill from the village of St. Paul de Vence, reached by negotiating a narrow twisting road, is the three-hundred-year-old farmhouse of James Baldwin. The red and white St. Paul city-limits sign spots the front-gate entrance to his home. To reach the two-story, light-brown stone-and-stucco house, one must follow a narrow cobblestone path umbrellaed by the trees. Entering this comfortable home, one is immediately struck by the commanding panoramic view from the dining-room windows. The scene opens out onto the valley below, now dotted with expensive villas. Mountains ring this picturesque valley; it is a beautiful, serene setting.

When I was taken to see Jimmy, who had been moved from the ground-floor wing of the house where he slept and worked to another bedroom that was very dark, I was shocked by his frail and weakened condition. I quickly hugged him and kissed the top of his head. I held him close for a long moment partly because I loved this man and also because I didn't want him to notice the sadness that had welled up into my eyes. But remembering that David had admonished me to "act normally," I quickly pulled myself together and told Jimmy how happy I was to see him. He smiled that brilliant smile of his, his large eyes bright and inquisitive, like a child. He told me in a very weak voice that he was convalescing and tired, but would come out to greet me properly in about two or three hours. Then those bright luminous owl eyes burned deeply into mine, as if seeking some clue, some sign that would give him a hint as to the seriousness of his condition. They probed for a moment and then released me from their questioning fire.

I was relieved when David led me out of the darkened house. I will never forget that image of Jimmy weakly sitting there, the feel of his now-wispy hair scratching my face when I hugged him, the birdlike frailty of his ravaged body and the parting telescopic image of him dressed in a red and green plaid robe that all but swallowed him, his large head lolling from one side to the other as his longtime friend, painter Lucien Happersburger, lifted him to put him to bed. It was a profoundly sad and moving experience that is etched indelibly in my mind.

Many articles in the house caught my attention, most notably the many paintings and pieces of sculpture, among them the colorful paintings of the late African-American expatriate painter Beauford Delaney, who had been one of Jimmy's best friends. There were two other pieces that I

believed said very much about the political commitment
of the man. One, a black pen-and-ink drawing of Nelson
Mandela against an orange background, accompanied by a
poem, was framed and hung over the dining-room fireplace,
the most prominent place in the house. The other was an assemblage created by Jimmy's brother David in his honor. The
items in this work were each of distinct interest, but when
viewed as a composite, their political statement was obvious
and stunning. The centerpiece was the citation of the French
Legion of Honor, presented to James Baldwin in January 1986
by François Mitterand. Beneath the framed citation, on the
fireplace mantle and placed on each side of it, was a sword
and an old hunting rifle, both pointing towards the certifi-
cate. Framed by these two pieces and sitting on the mantle
was a black-and-white photograph of Jimmy, an abstract steel
sculpture of an Indian pointing a bow and arrow, two crystal
inkwells, a figure resembling a guitar, and an oversize ink pen
pointed directly toward the Legion of Honor citation. Later,
when I asked David about the significance of the assemblage,
he said, "It was my homage to my brother."

I, too, will miss Jimmy—his profound, courageous, and
penetrating observations of America, his writing and fully
lived life, which was bountiful and always represented those
things that were meaningful and right.

I conducted my interview with him over a period of two
days, whenever his physical condition allowed, and our con-
versations ranged over a variety of literary and political topics.
He could not finish our last session because of the pain that
overwhelmed him.

One of the last things he said to me was that he hoped

that I and the other writers would continue to be witnesses of our time; that we must speak out against institutionalized and individual tyranny wherever we found it. Because if left unchecked, it threatened to engulf and subjugate us all—the fire this time. And, of course, he is right. He is right—about racism, violence, and cynical indifference that characterize modern society, and especially the contemporary values that are dominant here in America today.

The following interview contains James Baldwin's last words for publication. Savor them, as I have, from this profoundly human spirit who altered the course of so many lives with his enormous talent, his deep commitment to justice, and his abiding love for humanity. He will be deeply missed.

BALDWIN: It all comes back now.

TROUPE: When did you first meet Miles?

BALDWIN: Oh, a long time ago, on West Seventy-seventh Street at his house.

TROUPE: What were the circumstances?

BALDWIN: I'm trying to remember. I was living on West End Avenue then, early sixties. What was I doing at his home? I hadn't met him, but I admired him very much. But I think I met him before that. Yes, I remember. I first met him in the Village, when he was playing at the Café Bohemia. Then I met him at Club Beverly, on Seventy-fifth Street. But that was a long time ago, too. But, I'm trying to remember what I was doing at Miles's house. I don't remember. Anyway, it was a Sunday afternoon and Miles had invited me, he was having a kind of brunch. So there I was, there in Miles's presence. It was, at first, overwhelming, because I'm really shy. I remember there being a whole lot of people. Miles was at the other end of the room. At first he was upstairs, invisible. Then he was downstairs talking to someone he knew as Moonbeam. Still, he was visible, but barely. Finally he was standing in the room, visible, and so I went over to him. Miles looked like

a little boy at the time, he looked about ten. So there I was
trying to figure out what to say. Finally I told him how much
I liked and admired him. I told him I liked his music very
much and he said something like, "Are you sure?" He kind of
smiled. Then he talked with me. Then we sort of knew each
other. So the ice had been broken, so that, ah, you know, how
it is with friends, though I don't know if he thinks of me as
a friend. I don't know what other people see. But I could see
that there was something in Miles and me which was very
much alike. I can see much of myself in Miles. And yet, I
don't know what it is, can't explain it, but I think it has something to do with extreme vulnerability.

TROUPE: Extreme vulnerability? In what sense?

BALDWIN: First of all, you know, with what we look like, being black, which means that in special ways we've been mal-
treated. See, we evolve a kind of mask, a kind of persona,
you know, to protect us from, ah, all these people who are
carnivorous and they think you're helpless. Miles does it one
way, I do it another.

TROUPE: How do you do it?

BALDWIN: I keep people away by seeming not to be afraid of
them, by moving fast.

TROUPE: And how does he do it?

BALDWIN: In his language, by saying "bitch." Miles said when
he saw me signing an autograph, "Why don't you tell the

motherfuckers to get lost? What the fuck makes you think I think you can read?" I never saw him very often, but there was always a kind of shorthand between us, that nothing would ever change between us. Like Miles has come to visit me, here in St. Paul on a number of occasions when he's over here in France, playing. And you know Miles doesn't visit people. And even when he visits, he never says much, he doesn't say anything. Not all the time, however; it depends on how the spirit moves him.

TROUPE: So he just shows.

BALDWIN: He just shows up here, knocks at the door. Sometimes he calls, but he may just show.

TROUPE: When was the last time?

BALDWIN: A couple of summers ago.

TROUPE: He called and said, "I'm coming."

BALDWIN: No. I think what happened, he was staying in Nice, so his French manager called and asked me to come and have dinner and cocktails. It was a nice night. And afterwards, he came back here.

TROUPE: He came out here?

BALDWIN: Yeah. We sat around and talked about nothing.

TROUPE: You think he came because he feels safe with you.

BALDWIN: Yeah. We talked about nothing and everything and we would have a little sip and we would talk about whatever. But I do the same with some people I know.

TROUPE: Why do you think he feels this way with you, since he's afraid of writers?

BALDWIN: I don't think Miles thinks of me as a writer. He knows I'm a writer, but he doesn't look at me that way. He doesn't look at me that way at all. I think he thinks of me as a brother, you know? In many ways I have the same difficulty as he has, in terms of the private and public life. In terms of the legend. It's difficult to be a legend. It's hard for me to recognize *me*. You spend a lot of time trying to avoid it. A lot of the time I've been through so many of the same experiences Miles has gone through. It's really something, to be a legend, unbearable. I could see it had happened to Miles. Again, it's unbearable, the way the world treats you is unbearable, and especially if you're black.

TROUPE: What is that?

BALDWIN: It's unbearable because time is passing and you are not your legend, but you're trapped in it. Nobody will let you out of it. Except other people who know what it is. But very few people have experienced it, know about it, and I think that can drive you mad; I know it can. It had a terrible effect on him and it had a terrible effect on me. And you don't see it coming.

TROUPE: You don't see it coming? Explain why?

BALDWIN: No way to see it.

TROUPE: How do you realize it?

BALDWIN: You have to be lucky. You have to have friends. I think at bottom you have to be serious. No one can point it out to you; you have to see it yourself. That's the only way you can act on it. And when it arrives it's a great shock.

TROUPE: To find out?

BALDWIN: It's a great shock to realize that you've been so divorced. So divorced from who you think you are—from who you really are. Who you think you are, you're not at all. The only thing is that Miles has got his horn and I've got my typewriter. We are both angry men.

TROUPE: I want to ask you what you were trapped in and how did you come to see it. I mean, did you come through friends?

BALDWIN: I know what you're saying but it's hard to answer, it's hard.

TROUPE: I know it's hard.

BALDWIN: I don't know how to answer that.

TROUPE: But you saw yourself trapped?

BALDWIN: I saw myself trapped. I think it happened to Miles, too.

TROUPE: What did you think you were, before you knew?

BALDWIN: Ah, that's even more interesting. I don't know who I thought I was. I was a witness, I thought. I was a very despairing witness, though, too. What I was actually doing was trying to avoid a certain estrangement, perhaps, an estrangement between myself and my generation. It was virtually complete, the estrangement was, in terms of what I might have thought and expected—my theories. About what I might have hoped—I'm talking now in terms of one's function as an artist. And the country itself being black and trying to deal with that.

TROUPE: Why do you think it occurred, that estrangement between your generation and the country?

BALDWIN: Well, because I was right. That's a strange way to put it.

TROUPE: That's not strange, at least not to me.

BALDWIN: I *was* right. I was right about what was happening in the country. What was about to happen to all of us really, one way or the other. And the choices people would have to make. And watching people make them and denying them at the same time. I began to feel more and more homeless in terms of the whole relationship between France and me and America, and *me* has always been a little painful, you know. Because my family's in America I will always go back. It couldn't have been a question in my mind unless it absolutely really came to that. But in the meantime you keep the door open and the price of keeping the door open was to actually be, in a sense, victimized by my own legend. You know, I was trying to tell the truth and it takes a long time to realize that you can't—that there's no point in going to the mat, so to speak, no point in going to Texas again. There's no point in saying this again. It's been said, and it's been said, and it's been said. It's been heard and not heard. You are a broken motor.

TROUPE: A broken motor?

BALDWIN: Yes. You're a running motor and you're repeating, you're repeating, you're repeating, and it causes a breakdown, lessening of will power. And sooner or later your will gives out, it has to. You're lucky if it is a physical matter. Most times it's spiritual. See, all this involves hiding from something else—not dealing with how lonely you are. And of course, at the very bottom it involves the terror of every artist confronted with what he or she has to do, you know, the next work. And everybody, in one way or another, and to some extent, tries to avoid it. And you avoid it more when you get older than you do when you're younger; still there's something terrifying about it, about doing the work. Something like that. But it happened to Miles sooner than it happened to me. I think for me it was lucky that it was physical, because it could have been mental.

TROUPE: It could have been mental?

BALDWIN: Yes. It could have been mental debilitation instead of my present physical one. I prefer the physical to the mental. Does that make sense?

TROUPE: It makes good sense, it makes fanastic sense. Now let me ask you something else. Now with Miles, you both were born close to each other?

BALDWIN: Just about. I think I'm a year older. I was born in '24.

TROUPE: He was born in '26. So, then, probably both of you, black men, geniuses, born close together, probably see the world very similar—you through your typewriter and him through his horn. Both vulnerable. So when you met you were brothers because you expected to meet each other or were you looking for each other?

BALDWIN: Yes. We were looking for each other. Neither he nor I would have said it that way but we were; we knew that the moment we saw each other.

TROUPE: You were hoping?

BALDWIN: Oh yes. That's why I was watching him before he watched me, you know.

TROUPE: But he knew you.

BALDWIN: He knew about me. Yes.

TROUPE: He knew you when he saw you.

BALDWIN: There's no question about that at all. We knew each other at once.

TROUPE: That's wonderful.

BALDWIN: Yes, it is, discovering someone very much like yourself. It was wonderful.

TROUPE: And that's a wonderful connection. Because he's also estranged somewhat from his musical generation.

BALDWIN: He has to be, at least it makes sense to me that he would be, because he's always trying to be on the cutting edge of his art. That's certainly true for me.

TROUPE: In the window of your eyes, you and Miles remind me of each other. It's a certain distinctive juju.

BALDWIN: Shit, I love that.

TROUPE: It's a certain distinctive juju that in Miles you recognize and you see a face that you have not seen before. And when I look at you and since I've always looked at you, I've always felt that. A certain juju, witch doctor, priest, high priest look of timelessness or representative of a certain tribe, point of view, mysticism, magic.

BALDWIN: That would cover my father certainly. He was not really my father, because I was born out of wedlock, but that's the difference, my father. He did give me something. Don't you see, he taught me how to fight. He taught me how to fight. But it would be better to say he taught me what to fight for. I was only fighting for safety, or for money at first. Then I fought to make you look at me. Because I was not born to be what someone said I was. I was not born to be defined by someone else, but by myself, and myself only.

TROUPE: So when you were younger, you didn't have the pen as a weapon, as a defense, a shield. How did you fight then?

BALDWIN: Any way I could.

TROUPE: What would you do?

BALDWIN: It's hard to remember. The pulpit was part of it, but that came later.

TROUPE: Before the pulpit.

BALDWIN: It was the streets.

TROUPE: How did you fight? Any way you could?

BALDWIN: Well, if you wanted to beat me up, okay. And, say, you were bigger than I was, you could do it, you could beat me, but you gonna have to do it every day.

TROUPE: Every day? Because you would fight to the death.

BALDWIN: You'd have to beat me up every single day. So then the question becomes which one of us would get tired first. And I knew it wouldn't be me.

TROUPE: You would always fight.

BALDWIN: Oh yes, indeed. So then the other person would have to begin to think, and to be bugged by this kid he had to beat up every day. And some days perhaps he just didn't feel like doing it. But he would have to, yeah, because he said he was going to do it. So then come beat me up. But of course something happened to him, something has to happen to him—because someone beating someone else up is not so easy either. Because I would be standing in the schoolyard with a lead pipe as a deterrent. So, you know, eventually, it was just too dangerous. People began to leave me alone. Some of the big boys who were my friends got together and decided that they had to protect me, you know? So that after that I was really protected. Because it was funny to them after a while. But that's what happened. That was the beginning of it and then later on it was cops, you know. It became just a nightmare. Especially cops. I knew that they knew that I was seven or eight or nine and they were just having fun with me. They wanted me to beg. And I couldn't beg, so I got my ass kicked. But I learned a lot, a lot about them. I learned there were very few who were humane; they just wanted you to say what they wanted you to say. They wanted to be confirmed in something by you. By your face, by your terror of them.

TROUPE: What about the pulpit, the idea of the pulpit? Would you talk about it as an idea?

BALDWIN: That's a very complex idea, really. I joined the Church, but my joining it was very complex, though I meant it, the purely religious part that is, the spiritual part. In a way that was very important to me, that whole time in the pulpit, because it gave me a kind of distance that was kind of respected; that was the reason I was in the pulpit, to put distance between people and myself. I began to see my people, so to speak, both ethnically and otherwise. And in the time that I was in the pulpit I learned a lot about my father. And later on, I thought, perhaps, I'd moved into the pulpit in order to arrest him. Because I thought that he had to be arrested, had to be stopped. He was having a terrible effect on everybody in the family. I could go as far as to say I thought he was crazy. But I knew with myself and the pulpit I cut out a lot of his power. He couldn't fight me in that arena. He fought me, but he couldn't fight me in that arena. And I say during that time that it taught me a lot about him and myself and about the people who were in the congregation, whom I couldn't lie to. And that was why I left the pulpit.

TROUPE: Is that where you started to learn about the truth? I mean you knew about the truth when you were talking about when you knew you weren't going to give in.

BALDWIN: I couldn't.

TROUPE: So then in the pulpit you learned another truth. And in the writing you take it . . .

BALDWIN: I knew that was where I had to go. That I was

not going to become another fat preacher, you know? I was not going to, ah, lie to my congregation. I was not allowed to do that. I couldn't believe in what I had anymore. I didn't believe in the Christian Church anymore, not the way I had; I no longer believed in its spirituality, its healing powers.

TROUPE: Oh? Was it the Christian Church that disturbed you?

BALDWIN: The way people treated each other. In the Church and outside, but especially in the Church.

TROUPE: How did they treat each other?

BALDWIN: Well, they were so self-righteous. They didn't come with real deep love, for example. The people in the Church were very cruel about many things.

TROUPE: How old were you when you were involved in the Church?

BALDWIN: Fourteen, fifteen.

TROUPE: Okay. I want you now to talk about two extraordinary women that your brother David told me about. Jeanne Fauré, who used to own the house you live in now, and Tintine. I want you, at first, if you can, to talk to me about how you came to this house. And how you came to receive the medal of honor.

BALDWIN: Oh, that's a long story.

TROUPE: I know. But can you talk about it, if you can, how she came to accept you, why she accepted you, and what it was that you saw in each other?

BALDWIN: I came here to St. Paul in 1970. It was after Malcolm X's and Martin Luther King's deaths, really. After Martin's death I sort of wandered and indeed didn't know where to go. I was in Turkey for a while, then I ended up here. I didn't want to leave; I had to. I ended up across the street from this house in a hotel. I came in the wintertime, nineteen years ago. Anyway, I and a friend of mine came down to St. Paul from Paris. We didn't have anything because it was terribly expensive at the hotel and so we settled here because at the time it also served as a roominghouse. Later I got sick, you know, and much of my family came over to see me. I rented almost all of the house. So I thought why not buy it. It was forty-three, forty-six thousand and I had been very ill so I didn't know how much longer I had to live. So I bought it. But Madame Fauré had offered to sell it to me.

TROUPE: This was earlier?

BALDWIN: Yes. When I first came, nineteen-some-odd years ago.

TROUPE: What was wrong with you, can you remember what was the illness?

BALDWIN: Nobody knew. Nobody knew. But anyway, I needed some money to buy the house. That occupied me for a while, that occupied me considerably. But I was just busy working. And I got to know Jeanne Fauré, who was a very strange lady, solitary, very strange.

TROUPE: How would you describe her strangeness?

BALDWIN: In her solitude. She was a kind of legend, she was very old, you know, quite. And anyway, she and I had very little in common, it seemed to me, except I liked her very much. She was a refugee from Algeria, raised in Algeria, I believe, and then the French had to leave. And she was very bitter about that. That meant we had very little in common politically. And very little in common in what I could see in any other way. And yet there was something else beneath that made her my friend. She decided to sell the house to me; she refused to sell it to anybody else.

TROUPE: She decided to sell the house to you? Why do you think she picked you? Do you know to this day?

BALDWIN: No.

TROUPE: Was it spiritual?

BALDWIN: Yes.

TROUPE: Cosmic.

BALDWIN: I wasn't the best candidate; in fact, I was the worst. Something in her, I don't know. We also had a very stormy relationship.

TROUPE: Stormy?

BALDWIN: Politically speaking, we did. In many other ways we did, too. She knew something I didn't know. She knew about Europe, she knew about civilization, she knew about responsibility. A million things that I as an American would not know, that were alien to me. And I was very slow to learn these things. In fact, it was a very expensive lesson, one that I haven't learned entirely just yet. But she was a valuable kind of guide and a kind of protection. And Tintine Roux was the old lady who ran La Colombe D'Or, which is a world-famous restaurant and inn. She became my guardian. I never lived in a small town before, which is not so easy, and she protected me. I could come in and have lunch at her restaurant. And I didn't realize it at first, that she had picked herself to be my protector.

TROUPE: What do you think she saw in you?

BALDWIN: I don't know.

TROUPE: What do you think?

BALDWIN: I knew Tintine liked me. Still, she must have thought I was crazy, you know, at least a little strange, in any event. But both these women liked me. It was as though they recognized where I came from. That I was a peasant, and I am. But I've only found this out over time.

TROUPE: Why do you say that?

BALDWIN: I'm a peasant because of where I really come from, you know. My background, my father, my mother, the line. Something of the peasant must be in all of my family. And that's where Madame Fauré and Tintine come from, too. And the color of my skin didn't add into it at all. Both these women were watching something else besides my color. And they protected me and loved me. They're both dead now and I miss them both terribly. Because with Jeanne I truly learned a lot from her, from her European optic in regard to others; but she also had an optic that came from Algeria. What I liked about it was that she was willing to be my guide; willing and unwilling: in fact, she was a hard guide. But mostly she was willing. And so it seemed like she was my guide to something else.

TROUPE: What?

BALDWIN: To a way of life, to a potential civilization she had seen only from a height.

TROUPE: Didn't they know about your fame?

BALDWIN: No, not really. They'd heard of me. But beyond that, nothing.

TROUPE: You were comfortable with that.

BALDWIN: Yes. Because my fame did not get in the way, because by the time they knew, it didn't make any difference. It was just one more aspect of this crazy kid. That's the best way to put it. They were my guides, and they were very good guides.

TROUPE: David told me a story about an incident that happened when her brother died, and Madame Fauré picked you to be at the head of the funeral procession.

BALDWIN: He told you that? Well, she was the last of kin and she made me lead her brother Louis's funeral procession. Yes, she did. She put her arm in mine and I had to lead. I had to. It was an incredible scene. I had to lead the funeral procession with her or she with me. It was fascinating.

TROUPE: I think it's a great image. Tell me about it. How did you feel?

BALDWIN: I was in a state of shock. I didn't know what to do. And of course the people of St. Paul were shocked, too. This was in either 1974 or '75. But I was in a state of shock. I didn't quite know what to think; in fact, the town was in a state of shock.

TROUPE: What was the reason?

BALDWIN: Well, they knew who I was by then, of course, but they couldn't understand why I was representing the family. When we were at the cemetery everybody had to say goodbye to me, too. Because I was standing there with her at the head of the family, under the gates of the cemetery. Because what it meant, symbolically speaking, is that I was the next in line, when she died. That's what it meant.

TROUPE: Do you think that could have happened in America?

BALDWIN: I can't imagine where. I really cannot imagine where.

TROUPE: So in a sense that was a comforting, human experience. A remarkable spiritual connection, bond.

BALDWIN: A very great thing, very great. At least for me. I want to write about it one day. Yes, sometime I'll have to talk about it.

TROUPE: When you received the Legion of Honor of France, who did you take with you to the ceremony?

BALDWIN: David came over. Jeanne Fauré was there and my house-keeper Valerie was there too.

TROUPE: Why did you pick them?

BALDWIN: Because they had seen me through so much and I'd promised to take Jeanne and Valerie to Paris one day. Jeanne had been to Paris but she hadn't been there for a long time. I thought that would be nice for her to go. So I took them and because I owed it to them, but especially to Jeanne Fauré. Because she'd seen me through.

TROUPE: And how did she feel?

BALDWIN: She was very proud. She didn't say anything to me; she never said much to me about it. But I could see it—how proud she was—in her face, in her eyes.

TROUPE: What year was this?

BALDWIN: Last year, 1986.

TROUPE: Was that right before she died?

BALDWIN: Yes. She died in the winter of 1987.

TROUPE: What month was that?

BALDWIN: I received the award in June, and she died in January 1987.

TROUPE: And how did you feel with her being there?

BALDWIN: I was very pleased. It was very nice. It was something that gave her a great pleasure and that meant a lot to me.

TROUPE: I thought that was a great story when he told me. I said I was definitely going to ask you about that. Because I thought that was fundamentally fantastic and so fundamentally, in a sense, spiritually right; but it's something which you don't expect to happen.

BALDWIN: No, you don't, not at all.

TROUPE: Who gave you the award?

BALDWIN: The president, the president of France, François Mitterrand. The ceremony was at the Élysée in Paris.

TROUPE: What other people received the award that year?

BALDWIN: Leonard Bernstein. Leonard Bernstein and me. It was a very nice ceremony, very nice.

TROUPE: Okay. Let's change the subject and talk about some writers. What is your opinion of Amiri Baraka?

BALDWIN: I remember the first time I met Amiri Baraka, who was then LeRoi Jones. I was doing *The Amen Corner* and he was a student at Howard University. I liked him right away. He was a pop-eyed little boy, a poet. He showed me a couple of his poems. I liked them very much. And then he came to New York a couple of years later. He came to New York when I came back to New York from Paris. And by this time I knew the business. I'd been through the fucking business by that time. I was a survivor. And I remember telling him that his agent wanted him to become the young James Baldwin. But I told him, "You're not the young James Baldwin. There's only

one James Baldwin and you are LeRoi Jones and there's only
one LeRoi Jones. Don't let them run this game on us, you
know? You're LeRoi Jones, I'm James Baldwin. And we're going to need each other." That's all I said. He didn't believe it
then but time took care of that.

TROUPE: He believes it now.

BALDWIN: Yes, he knows it now.

TROUPE: What person has hurt you the most recently?

BALDWIN: Ishmael Reed.

TROUPE: Why?

BALDWIN: Because he is a great poet and it seemed to
be beneath him, his anger and his contempt for me,
which were both real and not real. He ignored me for so
long and then he called me a cocksucker, you know what
I mean? It's boring. But I always did say he was a great
poet, a great writer. But that does not mean I can put up
with being insulted by him every time I see him, which
I won't.

TROUPE: What do you think about Toni Morrison?

BALDWIN: Toni's my ally and it's really probably too complex
to get into. She's a black woman writer, which in the public
domain makes it more difficult to talk about.

TROUPE: Have you read *Beloved*?

BALDWIN: Not yet. She sent it to me but I haven't read it yet.

TROUPE: What do you think are her gifts?

BALDWIN: Her gift is in allegory. *Tar Baby* is an allegory. In fact, all her novels are. But they're hard to talk about in public. That's where you get in trouble because her books and allegory are not always what it seems to be about. I was too occupied with my recent illness to deal with *Beloved*. But in general she's taken a myth, or she takes what seems to be a myth, and turns it into something else. I don't know how to put this—*Beloved* could be about the story of truth. She's taken a whole lot of things and turned them upside down. Some of them—you recognize the truth in it. I think that Toni's very painful to read.

TROUPE: Painful?

BALDWIN: Yes.

TROUPE: Why?

BALDWIN: Because it's always or most times a horrifying allegory; but you recognize that it works. But you don't really want to march through it. Sometimes people have a lot against Toni, but she's got the most believing story of everybody—this rather elegant matron, whose intentions really are serious and, according to some people, lethal.

TROUPE: I remember you saying that Alex Haley's *Roots* had another title. What was it called first?

BALDWIN: It was called *Before the Anger*. But let me change the subject and just say this. It's very important for white Americans to believe their version of the black experience. That's why they have white and black commentators telling all those lies about us. You see, it's very important for the nigger to suffer. Therefore, they, white people, can feel guilty. Therefore, they can do something about it in their own good time. Let me again explain further. Once, after I published *Go Tell It on the Mountain* and *Giovanni's Room*, my publisher, Knopf, told me I was a "Negro writer" and that I "reached a certain audience." So, they told me, "you cannot afford to alienate that audience. This new book will ruin your career because you're not writing about the same things and in the same manner as you were before and we won't publish this book as a favor to you."

TROUPE: As a favor to you?

BALDWIN: So I told them fuck you. My editor, whose name I won't mention here, is dead now, poor man. Later on, Bennett Cerf and I tangled too, but that was about a Christmas boycott of books we were planning.

TROUPE: So what did they say after you told them "fuck you"?

BALDWIN: I told them that I needed a boat ticket. So I took a boat to England with my book and I sold it in England before

I sold it in America. You see, whites want black writers to mostly deliver something as if it were an official version of the black experience. But the vocabulary won't hold it, simply. No true account, really, of black life can be held, can be contained in the American vocabulary. As it is, the only way that you can deal with it is by doing great violence to the assumptions on which the vocabulary is based. But they won't let you do that. And when you go along, you find yourself very quickly painted into a corner; you've written yourself into a corner. Because you can't compromise as a writer. By the time I left America in 1948, I had written myself into a corner as I perceived it. The book reviews and the short essays had led me to a place where I was on a collision course totally with the truth; it was the way I was operating. It was only a matter of time before I'd simply be destroyed by it. And no amount of manipulation of vocabulary or part would have spared me. It's like I think that Al Murray and Ralph Ellison are totally trapped. It's sad, because they're both trapped in the same way, and they're both very gifted writers. Ralph certainly, and Al, I thought. But you can't do anything with America unless you are willing to dissect it. You certainly cannot hope to fit yourself into it; nothing fits into it, not your past, not your present. The *Invisible Man* is fine as far as it goes until you ask yourself who's invisible to whom? You know, what is this dichotomy supposed to do? Are we invisible before each other? And invisible why, and by what system can one hope to be invisible? I don't know how anything in American life is worthy of this sacrifice. And further, I don't see anything in American life—for myself—to aspire to. Nothing at all. It's all so very false. So shallow, so plastic, so morally and ethically corrupt.

TROUPE: We were talking once about the claustrophobia among writers. You said you prefer actors and painters to writers.

BALDWIN: Yes. Well, first of all when I was coming up there weren't any writers that I knew. Langston Hughes was far away. The first writer I met was Richard Wright and he was much older than me. And the people I knew were people like Beauford Delaney and the women who hung out with him; it was a whole world that was not literary. That came later; then it wasn't literary. It came later in Paris, with Sartre and others. But there was something else. And in Paris it had nothing whatsoever to do with race for one thing. It was another kind of freedom there altogether. It had nothing to do with literature. But we can't talk about that. But when I looked back on it years and years later, looked back at myself on the American literary scene, I could see that what almost happened to me was an attempt to make myself fit in, so to speak, to wash myself clean for the American literary academy.

TROUPE: You mean they wanted you scrubbed and squeaky clean?

BALDWIN: Exactly. You have to be scrubbed and squeaky clean and then there's nothing left of you. Let me tell you a story. When Ralph Ellison won the National Book Award in 1953 for *Invisible Man*, I was up for it the next year, in 1954, for *Go Tell It on the Mountain*. But at the time I was far from scrubbed. I didn't win. Then, years later, someone who was on the jury told me that since Ralph won it the year before, they couldn't give it to a Negro two years in a row. Now, isn't that something?

TROUPE: A judge told you that? Can you tell us his name?

BALDWIN: No, I wouldn't want to do that.

TROUPE: Okay. Do you have any comments on Norman Mailer?

BALDWIN: Well, the answer to that question is very short and very simple. Not simple, but short. Norman decided not to be a writer. He decided to be a celebrity instead and that's what he is now. Now let me tell you a story about Norman. Out of my father's first marriage there is a sister and a couple of sons, you know, a few sons. My sister had a brother who lives in California. He's a senior citizen now. But he lived with Norman Mailer when Norman was writing *The White Negro*. He was taking the pages out of Norman's typewriter, changing his clothes—they wore the same clothes, exchanged cars, and his car was better than Norman's at the time. He was like the second husband in a way. They lived together. They lived close together. Norman doesn't know I know this. No one knows this. This story took place in the forties, the early forties, in California. I've kept quiet about this all these years that Norman was living with one of my stepbrothers when he wrote the book. No one knows it, though. You're the first one, outside of the family, that I have mentioned it to. His name is

Osby Mitchell. Osby did something in show business, hung out with Frank Sinatra, Charlie Chaplin, that crowd.

TROUPE: Okay. That's something. Now, what do you think of the great praise you have received in France for *Just Above My Head* that it has gotten in translation. How does that make you feel?

BALDWIN: As you know, the French call the book *Harlem Quartet*. I don't know how to answer that, Quincy, because it was written here almost ten years ago. It was the hardest book I'd ever written until then.

TROUPE: Why?

BALDWIN: I had to face my own legends, too.

TROUPE: Which were?

BALDWIN: It had something to do with my brothers, my relationship to my brothers. And that implied relationship to my whole life, really. The key to one's life is always in a lot of unexpected places. I tried to deal with what I was most afraid of. That's why the vehicle of the book is music. Because music was and is my salvation. And when the book was done, I was glad it was over. It got the usual stormy reception in America, but by that time I was used to it. In any case, by that time I was in a different kind of trouble altogether. The reception of *Harlem Quartet* here in France didn't mean as much as it might have meant if I had gotten the praise earlier. I never thought I'd see the book again. But its translation came about after my book on the Atlanta murders was published here in France. It was hard to get the Atlanta book published in America for complex and political reasons.

TROUPE: Can you talk about them?

BALDWIN: I don't quite know what they are. It's difficult for me to talk about a book that involves a possible lawsuit. It's just another example of American business, the ways in which Americans, the American publishers, attempt to control and to demolish the American writer, regardless of color, but especially a black one. I had to fight that, so I brought the book here. And it was published by Stock. And it did better than anyone thought it would do in France. So Stock already had a contract for *Just Above My Head* (*Harlem Quartet*). And so they published it. Stock had gone through all kinds of publishing problems—it had gone through a breakup and a reorganization. The Atlanta book won a couple of awards, and a German writer and I won the Human Rights Award of France two years ago, in 1985. But the German writer, poor man, had to leave Germany. Anyway, behind all of this came this book *Just Above My Head*, or *Harlem Quartet*. And I think that the French for the first time really looked at my writing; the Atlanta book was something of a shock to them.

TROUPE: Why?

BALDWIN: Because it demolishes, so to speak, the American myth of integration, you know, by using Atlanta, which is supposed to be the model of integration in the Deep South, and exposes it for what it is; shit, you know? So the French reader goes through all of that in terms of those twenty-eight dead black children. And so it was a shock, you know. And it sort of set up, I don't know what, exactly, but it did set up expectations, or fears, whatever for the novel. It may have set up an audience for the novel. And so *Just Above My Head* turns out to be somewhat of a revelation for the French. So you know, I'm considered somewhat of an intellectual in Paris. I mean in France. For a black writer, you know? Essentially as an essayist. But the novel was a great revelation; it gave me another kind of reputation altogether. Because now, instead of an essayist, what they saw in me was a novelist. I'm much better known as an essayist in France and elsewhere, too, than I am as a novelist. Before, the translations of my novels in France have been so bad. But this was a good translation, a marvelous translation, which makes a tremendous difference. And the subject, my handling of the subject, they liked. So it's simply a matter of something happening at the right time, and that can never be foreseen, you know.

TROUPE: What's the award *Harlem Quartet* is up for now?

BALDWIN: The best foreign novel published in France, the Prix Femina. We will know about that in a week.

TROUPE: Let me ask you about the difficulty the American press and critics might have had in getting into your fiction.

BALDWIN: Well, probably the American legend of black life. It's one thing to be aware of a Miles Davis and quite another thing to know where he comes from and what sustains him. Hollywood should be sued for libel, it's true. So that the book, my book, and others come as a direct opposition of the myth by Americans of black life and black music. It's not like what they, the press and critics, say it is, not at all. But the books prove them wrong, so they ignore the books. You see what I mean? Like I very much liked the film *Round Midnight*, which is a very important film. It fills in something that is important in our lives, a gap that was once there, that one might have thought about but didn't know about.

TROUPE: Why do you say it's important?

BALDWIN: Well, first of all, the personality of Dexter Gordon, he gives at least a reading of what happens to the musician. The black musician inside the music industry in Paris, you know? The ruin that they met which they brought with them and which wasn't brought about by Paris.

TROUPE: You mean the black musicians brought the ruin with them?

BALDWIN: Yes, that's precisely what I mean. And *Round Midnight* makes that point in some ways very clearly.

TROUPE: Can you talk about the neglect of the black painter Beauford Delaney?

BALDWIN: That's hard to do because people are still lying about Beauford. Let's talk about that over supper.

TROUPE: Okay. You said something to me once about how people shouldn't be jealous of someone's success. Do you recall that?

BALDWIN: Well, what I was really trying to say was that people don't know what it is sometimes to be very successful. Don't know what it is. What I meant to say was that you can't be jealous of somebody else's success because you have no idea what it means, you know? It looks like success to you, but you're not the one that's paying for it.

TROUPE: And there's a price?

BALDWIN: Of course there's a price, are you kidding? It's definitely not easy. It's rough. But for most great black writers in general, "they"—meaning white and black Americans—won't read us until they have nothing else to read.

TROUPE: Why do you think that is?

BALDWIN: Well, because of the entire way of American life, the marrow of the American bone. Now today it's a *fait accompli*. There's nothing to be done about it. The whole American optic in terms of reality is based on the necessity of keeping black people out of it. We are nonexistent. Except according to their terms, and their terms are unacceptable.

TROUPE: Let me ask you this, since you said that. How do you look at the American society as it was during Dr. King's time and now? Any changes? Do you think it is worse, or what?

BALDWIN: Certainly, in my opinion, it's worse. I'm not sure it's the society, I don't know what it is now.

TROUPE: What do you think that Ronald Reagan represents to white America?

BALDWIN: Ronald Reagan represents the justification of their history, their sense of innocence. He means the justification of *Birth of a Nation*. The justification, in short, of being white.

TROUPE: How do you think white Americans feel now that they're in this economic crisis?

BALDWIN: They're not thinking about it.

TROUPE: What?

BALDWIN: They're not thinking about it. Americans don't think of such things. They try and get out of it. They hope it'll go away. And luckily they began to realize that maybe Reagan has to go, too. But they hope it all goes away. Because it's like a bad dream for them.

TROUPE: Won't they do anything to help it go away?

BALDWIN: No. Because they don't know how. They don't know how they got into it or, worse, won't recognize how. I don't know. They don't know how they got into the chaos of their cities, for example. But they did it. Now how and why did they do it? They did it because they wanted their children to be safe, to be raised safely. So they set up their communities so that they wouldn't have to go to school with black children, whom they fear, and that dictates the structure of their cities, the chaos of their cities and the danger in which they live.

TROUPE: "They" being white.

BALDWIN: "They" being white and their believing that they're white. But they did it; niggers didn't do it. They did it. Inch by inch, stone by stone, decree by decree. Now their kids are deeply lost and they can't even blame it now on the nigger, you know what I mean?

TROUPE: Yes.

BALDWIN: That's what happened, I don't care who says what. I watched it happen, I know because I watched it happen. And all this, because they want to be white. And why do they want to be white? Because it's the only way to justify the slaughter of the Indians and enslaving the blacks—they're trapped. And nothing, nothing will spring the trap, nothing. Now they're really trapped because the world is present. And the world is not white and America is not the symbol of civilization. Neither is England. Neither is France. Something else is happening which will engulf them by and by. You, Quincy, will be here, but I'll be gone. It's the only hope the world has, that the notion of the supremacy of Western hegemony and civilization be contained.

TROUPE: Do you have any feelings about yuppies?

BALDWIN: I saw them coming. I knew them. They can't, I'm afraid, be taught anything.

TROUPE: You don't think they can be taught anything?

BALDWIN: No. Because you can't be taught anything if you think you know everything already, that something else—greed, materialism, and consuming—is more important to your life. You know, I taught the yuppies before they were called yuppies. And then what happened to them, really? Perfectly sound young men came out of college, went to work for Nixon, and were hardened criminals on Wall Street before you knew it. Now, is it true or not?

TROUPE: It's true.

BALDWIN: And here I've only mentioned Nixon. But it's true for Reagan, too. So that's that. It's the fiber of the nation, unfortunately.

JAMES BALDWIN (1924–1987) was an American novelist, essayist, playwright, and social critic. Born in Harlem, as a teenager Baldwin got to know members of the Harlem Renaissance, including the painter Beauford Delaney, and the Greenwich Village literary world, and began his career writing reviews and short stories. In 1948, he left New York for Paris, where he completed his first novel, *Go Tell It on the Mountain* (1953). His other major works include *Giovanni's Room*, *The Fire Next Time*, and *Notes of a Native Son*. He was deeply involved in the civil rights movement in the sixties. He spent his later years in the town of St. Paul de Vence on the French Riviera, where he died of cancer at the age of sixty-three.

LOUIS "STUDS" TERKEL (1912–2008) was a radio broadcaster and historian, known especially for his oral histories on topics including World War II, the Depression, race, jazz, and labor. His weekly radio interview progam, *The Studs Terkel Show*, ran on Chicago's 98.7 WFMT from 1952 to 1997.

JULIUS LESTER is the author of more than forty award-winning books for children and adults, as well contributing essays and criticism to numerous publications. He was a member of the faculty at University of Massachusetts, Amherst, from 1971 to 2003, where he taught English, comparative literature, Afro-American studies, and Judaic studies.

RICHARD GOLDSTEIN is the former executive editor of *The Village Voice*, where he wrote regularly on counterculture, music, and LGBT issues for more than thirty years. His memoir of his life in the sixties, *Another Little Piece of My Heart*, will be published by Bloomsbury in April 2015.

QUINCY TROUPE is a poet and editor, and professor emeritus at University of California, San Diego. He is the author of many collections of poetry, among them *Snake-Back Solos: Selected Poems 1969–1977* and *Transcircularities: New and Selected Poems*. He is the co-author of *Miles: The Autobiography of Miles Davis*, as well as the author of a memoir, *Miles and Me*.

THE LAST INTERVIEW SERIES

KURT VONNEGUT: THE LAST INTERVIEW

"I think it can be tremendously refreshing if a creator of literature has something on his mind other than the history of literature so far. Literature should not disappear up its own asshole, so to speak."

$15.95 / $17.95 CAN
978-1-61219-090-7
ebook: 978-1-61219-091-4

LEARNING TO LIVE FINALLY: THE LAST INTERVIEW
JACQUES DERRIDA

"I am at war with myself, It's true, you couldn't possibly know to what extent . . . I say contradictory things that are, we might say, in real tension; they are what construct me, make me live, and will make me die."

translated by PASCAL-ANNE BRAULT and MICHAEL NAAS

$15.95 / $17.95 CAN
978-1-61219-094-5
ebook: 978-1-61219-032-7

ROBERTO BOLAÑO: THE LAST INTERVIEW

"Posthumous: It sounds like the name of a Roman gladiator, an unconquered gladiator. At least that's what poor Posthumous would like to believe. It gives him courage."

translated by SYBIL PEREZ and others

$15.95 / $17.95 CAN
978-1-61219-095-2
ebook: 978-1-61219-033-4

THE LAST INTERVIEW SERIES

DAVID FOSTER WALLACE: THE LAST INTERVIEW

"I don't know what you're thinking or what it's like inside you and you don't know what it's like inside me. In fiction... we can leap over that wall itself in a certain way."

$15.95 / $15.95 CAN
978-1-61219-206-2
ebook: 978-1-61219-207-9

JORGE LUIS BORGES: THE LAST INTERVIEW

"Believe me: the benefits of blindness have been greatly exaggerated. If I could see, I would never leave the house, I'd stay indoors reading the many books that surround me."

translated by KIT MAUDE

$15.95 / $15.95 CAN
978-1-61219-204-8
ebook: 978-1-61219-205-5

HANNAH ARENDT: THE LAST INTERVIEW

"There are no dangerous thoughts for the simple reason that thinking itself is such a dangerous enterprise."

$15.95 / $15.95 CAN
978-1-61219-311-3
ebook: 978-1-61219-312-0